Low Cholesterol Cookbook For Beginners

Explore an Abundance of Simple and Delicious Meals Along with Practical Advice to Adopt a Heart-Healthy Eating Plan and Significantly Enhance Your Cardiovascular Health

Adriana Piccio

Table of content

CHAPTER 1: UNDERSTANDING CHOLESTEROL 7

WHAT IS CHOLESTEROL? 7

TYPES OF CHOLESTEROL: LDL VS HDL 10

CHAPTER 2: BENEFITS OF A LOW CHOLESTEROL DIET 15

IMPROVEMENTS IN HEART HEALTH 15

REDUCED RISK OF CHRONIC DISEASES 17

ADDITIONAL BENEFITS TO OVERALL HEALTH 20

CHAPTER 3: PRINCIPLES OF A LOW CHOLESTEROL DIET 24

FOODS TO INCLUDE 24

FOODS TO AVOID 27

CHAPTER 4: LOW CHOLESTEROL BREAKFASTS 31

EASY RECIPES TO GET YOUR DAY OFF TO A GOOD START 31

   1. Avocado and Tomato Toast 31

   2. Berry Overnight Oats 31

   3. Spinach and Mushroom Egg White Omelette 32

   4. Greek Yogurt with Fresh Berries and Honey 33

   5. Quinoa Breakfast Bowl with Almonds and Bananas 34

   6. Whole Grain Pancakes with Blueberry Compote 34

   7. Chia Seed Pudding with Mango 35

   8. Apple and Cinnamon Steel-Cut Oats 36

   9. Veggie Scramble with Whole Wheat Toast 36

   10. Smoked Salmon and Avocado Bagel 37

   11. Cottage Cheese with Pineapple and Chia Seeds 37

   12. Low-Fat Greek Yogurt Parfait with Granola 38

   13. Whole Wheat English Muffin with Peanut Butter and Banana 38

   14. Tomato and Basil Frittata 39

   15. Oatmeal with Sliced Almonds and Dried Cranberries 39

   16. Sweet Potato and Black Bean Breakfast Burrito 40

   17. Lemon Ricotta Pancakes 41

   18. Zucchini and Carrot Muffins 41

   19. Tofu Scramble with Spinach and Mushrooms 42

   20. Green Tea Infused Oatmeal 43

SMOOTHIES AND QUICK OPTIONS 44

21. Green Detox Smoothie...44

22. Berry Blast Smoothie..44

23. Tropical Mango Smoothie..45

24. Spinach and Avocado Smoothie..45

25. Pineapple and Kale Smoothie...46

26. Blueberry and Almond Milk Smoothie..46

27. Strawberry Banana Smoothie...47

28. Apple and Carrot Smoothie..47

29. Beetroot and Ginger Smoothie...48

30. Protein-Packed Smoothie with Chia Seeds...48

CHAPTER 5: HEALTHY LUNCHES..49

TASTY AND NUTRITIOUS RECIPES FOR LUNCH 49

31. Grilled Chicken and Quinoa Salad 49

32. Lentil and Vegetable Soup 50

33. Chickpea and Spinach Stew..51

34. Grilled Veggie Wrap with Hummus 52

35. Turkey and Avocado Sandwich...52

36. Asian-Inspired Tofu Salad 53

37. Greek Salad with Lemon Vinaigrette 53

38. Black Bean and Corn Salad 54

39. Zucchini Noodles with Pesto 54

40. Tomato and Basil Soup 55

41. Spinach and Strawberry Salad with Poppy Seed Dressing 55

42. Baked Falafel with Tahini Sauce...56

43. Stuffed Bell Peppers with Quinoa 57

44. Cucumber and Dill Yogurt Salad...57

45. Mixed Greens with Grilled Shrimp..58

46. Roasted Beet and Arugula Salad...58

47. Avocado and Black Bean Tacos 59

48. Vegetable Sushi Rolls...59

49. Whole Wheat Pasta Salad with Cherry Tomatoes and Feta 60

50. Kale and Sweet Potato Salad 60

CHAPTER 6: HEALTHY AND FLAVORFUL DINNERS...62

EVENING MEALS THE WHOLE FAMILY WILL ENJOY 62

52. Quinoa-Stuffed Bell Peppers 63

53. Grilled Chicken with Mango Salsa 64

54. Vegetarian Chili with Black Beans...64

55. Baked Cod with a Garlic Herb Crust 65

56. Tofu Stir-Fry with Broccoli and Peppers..66

57. Spaghetti Squash with Marinara Sauce 66

58. Moroccan Chickpea Stew 67

59. Roasted Turkey Breast with Sweet Potatoes 68

60. Vegetable Paella 68

61. Grilled Portobello Mushrooms 69

62. Herb-Crusted Tilapia 70

63. Baked Eggplant Parmesan..70

64. Chicken and Vegetable Kebabs 71

65. Stuffed Acorn Squash 72

66. Slow-Cooked Beef and Vegetable Stew 73

67. Shrimp and Avocado Salad 73

68. Cauliflower Rice Stir-Fry 74

69. Spicy Lentil Curry 75

70. Balsamic Glazed Chicken 75

71. Miso-Glazed Salmon 76

72. Zucchini Lasagna...77

73. Turkey Meatballs with Marinara Sauce 77

74. Vegan Shepherd's Pie 78

75. Grilled Vegetable Platter with Hummus 79

CHAPTER 7: SNACKS AND SNACKING 80

QUICK AND EASY RECIPES 80

77. Baked Sweet Potato Fries...80

78. Apple Slices with Almond Butter 81

79. Edamame with Sea Salt...81

80. Greek Yogurt Dip with Cucumber Slices 81

81. Roasted Chickpeas 82

82. Fresh Fruit Salad 82

83. Cottage Cheese with Pineapple 83

84. Celery Sticks with Low-Fat Cream Cheese 83

85. Air-Popped Popcorn with Nutritional Yeast 84

86. Avocado Toast Bites 84

87. Mixed Nuts and Dried Fruit Mix 85

88. Rice Cakes with Hummus and Cherry Tomatoes 85

89. Berry and Spinach Smoothie...85

90. Dark Chocolate and Almonds... 86

CHAPTER 8: DELICIOUS AND HEALTHY DESSERTS. 87

DESSERTS THAT SATISFY WITHOUT COMPROMISING HEALTH 87

92. Berry Chia Seed Pudding.. 87

93. Baked Apples with Cinnamon.. 88

94. Greek Yogurt with Honey and Walnuts 88

95. Banana and Oat Cookies.. 89

96. Mango Sorbet 89

97. Almond Flour Brownies... 90

98. Coconut and Lime Energy Balls 90

99. Frozen Yogurt Bark with Berries 91

100. Apple and Blueberry Crisp... 91

101. Dark Chocolate Covered Strawberries 92

102. Pineapple and Mint Sorbet 93

103. Lemon and Poppy Seed Muffins 93

104. Baked Pears with Walnuts 94

105. Raspberry and Almond Parfait 94

CHAPTER 9: PRACTICAL TIPS FOR MAINTAINING THE DIET 95

21-DAY MEAL PLAN 95

SHOPPING LIST 98

Chapter 1: Understanding Cholesterol

Cholesterol is a term that often sparks worry, yet it plays an indispensable role in our bodies. This waxy, fat-like substance is found in every cell and is crucial for producing hormones, vitamin D, and bile acids that aid digestion. However, cholesterol's dual nature—being both essential and potentially harmful—makes understanding its different types critical. By delving into what cholesterol is and differentiating between low-density lipoprotein (LDL) and high-density lipoprotein (HDL), we can better grasp how to manage it effectively to maintain heart health and overall well-being.

What is cholesterol?

Cholesterol, a term that often evokes concern and confusion, is a vital substance found in every cell of the human body. It's a waxy, fat-like compound that travels through the bloodstream and plays essential roles in various bodily functions. Despite its negative reputation, cholesterol is not inherently bad. In fact, it's crucial for maintaining overall health, serving as a building block for cell membranes, producing hormones, and assisting in the synthesis of vitamin D and bile acids that aid in digesting fat.

At its core, cholesterol is a lipid, which means it is a type of fat. However, unlike the fats we typically consume in our diets, cholesterol is primarily produced by the liver. The body makes all the cholesterol it needs, but it can also be ingested through animal-based foods like meat, dairy products, and eggs. This dual source can sometimes lead to an imbalance, which is where problems begin to arise.

In our bodies, cholesterol is transported through the bloodstream by molecules called lipoproteins. These lipoproteins are essentially carriers that package cholesterol and other fats, enabling them to travel around the body. Without these carriers, cholesterol would not be able to move within the watery environment of our blood.

Now, cholesterol itself is neither good nor bad. However, the way it is transported and its levels in the blood can lead to health implications. This brings us to the different types of lipoproteins that carry cholesterol, which are crucial to understanding cholesterol's role in health and disease.

Low-density lipoprotein (LDL) and high-density lipoprotein (HDL) are the two main types of cholesterol carriers in the blood. They have distinct functions and impacts on health, often referred to as "bad" and "good" cholesterol, respectively.

Low-density lipoprotein (LDL) is often labeled as "bad" cholesterol because it can lead to the buildup of cholesterol in the arteries. This process, known as atherosclerosis, can result in the narrowing and hardening of the arteries, impeding blood flow. If an artery becomes blocked, it can lead to severe cardiovascular events such as heart attacks or strokes. LDL carries cholesterol from the liver to the cells, but when there's too much LDL cholesterol in the blood, it can accumulate on the walls of the arteries, forming plaques that narrow and harden these vital pathways.

Conversely, high-density lipoprotein (HDL) is known as "good" cholesterol. HDL's primary role is to carry cholesterol away from the arteries and back to the liver, where it's processed and eliminated from the body. This reverse transport process helps protect against the buildup of cholesterol in the arteries, thus reducing the risk of cardiovascular disease. In simple terms, while LDL delivers cholesterol to cells, HDL helps remove it from the bloodstream, providing a cleansing effect.

Cholesterol's significance extends beyond these basic functions. It's essential for the formation of steroid hormones, which include sex hormones like estrogen and testosterone. These hormones regulate a variety of bodily processes, from reproductive functions to maintaining muscle mass and bone density. Additionally, cholesterol is involved in the production of cortisol, a hormone that helps the body respond to stress and maintain energy balance.

Another vital role of cholesterol is in the synthesis of bile acids. Bile acids are necessary for the digestion and absorption of dietary fats and fat-soluble vitamins like vitamins A, D, E, and K. Without sufficient cholesterol, the body would struggle to process these nutrients, leading to deficiencies and related health issues.

It's important to understand that cholesterol is a natural and necessary substance. Problems arise not from its presence but from its imbalance. Modern lifestyles, characterized by poor dietary choices, lack of exercise, and high stress levels, can disrupt the delicate balance of cholesterol in the body, leading to elevated LDL levels and reduced HDL levels. This imbalance can set the stage for cardiovascular diseases, which are among the leading causes of death globally.

Dietary habits play a significant role in cholesterol levels. Consuming high amounts of saturated fats, trans fats, and cholesterol-rich foods can increase LDL cholesterol levels. Foods such as fatty cuts of meat, full-fat dairy products, and processed foods like baked goods and fried items are typical culprits. On the other hand, a diet rich in fruits, vegetables, whole grains, and healthy fats, such as those found in nuts, seeds, and fish, can help maintain healthy cholesterol levels. These foods not only provide essential nutrients but also contain compounds like fiber and antioxidants that support cardiovascular health.

Exercise is another critical factor in managing cholesterol levels. Regular physical activity helps raise HDL cholesterol levels while lowering LDL cholesterol levels and triglycerides, another type of fat in the blood. Activities like walking, jogging, cycling, and swimming can significantly impact cholesterol levels and overall heart health. Additionally, maintaining a healthy weight through a balanced diet and regular exercise can further reduce the risk of cholesterol-related health issues.

While genetics also play a role in an individual's cholesterol levels, lifestyle choices have a profound impact. Some people may have a genetic predisposition to high cholesterol, making it even more crucial to adopt heart-healthy habits. For these individuals, lifestyle modifications combined with medical interventions, such as cholesterol-lowering medications, may be necessary to manage their cholesterol levels effectively.

In conclusion, cholesterol is an indispensable component of the human body, integral to numerous physiological processes. Understanding cholesterol and its functions helps demystify its often misunderstood nature. By recognizing the importance of balance and the impact of lifestyle choices, individuals can take proactive steps to maintain healthy cholesterol levels and support their cardiovascular health.

Types of cholesterol: LDL vs HDL

When we talk about cholesterol, we often encounter terms like LDL and HDL. These acronyms stand for low-density lipoprotein and high-density lipoprotein, respectively. Understanding the difference between these two types is crucial for grasping how cholesterol functions in the body and why managing its levels is essential for maintaining heart health.

Low-Density Lipoprotein (LDL)

LDL, commonly referred to as "bad" cholesterol, plays a significant role in the development of cardiovascular diseases. LDL's primary function is to transport cholesterol from the liver, where it is produced or ingested through diet, to the various cells throughout the body. Cells use cholesterol for several purposes, including building cell membranes and producing hormones. However, problems arise when there is an excess of LDL cholesterol in the bloodstream.

Imagine LDL as a delivery truck carrying cholesterol to the cells. When there are too many trucks on the road, traffic jams can occur. Similarly, when there is too much LDL in the blood, it can lead to the buildup of cholesterol on the walls of arteries, forming plaques. This condition is known as atherosclerosis. These plaques can narrow the arteries, restricting blood flow and increasing the risk of heart attacks and strokes. Additionally, if a plaque ruptures, it can create a blood clot, which can further block the artery and lead to severe cardiovascular events.

The body requires a certain amount of LDL to function properly, but maintaining the right balance is key. Factors such as a diet high in saturated and trans fats, lack of exercise, smoking, and genetic predisposition can all contribute to elevated LDL levels. To manage LDL cholesterol, it is recommended to adopt a heart-healthy diet, engage in regular physical activity, and, if necessary, take cholesterol-lowering medications prescribed by a healthcare provider.

High-Density Lipoprotein (HDL)

HDL, known as "good" cholesterol, has a protective effect on the cardiovascular system. HDL's primary role is to transport cholesterol away from the arteries and back to the liver, where it can be processed and eliminated from the body. Think of HDL as a cleanup crew that helps remove excess cholesterol from the bloodstream, thus preventing the formation of plaques and reducing the risk of heart disease.

Higher levels of HDL cholesterol are associated with a lower risk of cardiovascular diseases. This is because HDL helps maintain the balance by ensuring that excess cholesterol is transported out of the arteries. Several lifestyle choices can help increase HDL levels, including engaging in regular exercise, consuming healthy fats like those found in olive oil and fatty fish, quitting smoking, and maintaining a healthy weight.

HDL's ability to counterbalance the effects of LDL makes it an essential component of cholesterol management. It's like having a team of skilled workers who keep the roads clear and traffic flowing smoothly, ensuring that the delivery trucks (LDL) do not cause blockages and accidents in the form of heart attacks or strokes.

The Balance Between LDL and HDL

The interplay between LDL and HDL cholesterol is vital for cardiovascular health. While LDL is necessary for transporting cholesterol to cells, HDL ensures that excess cholesterol is removed from the bloodstream. Maintaining an optimal balance between these two types of cholesterol can significantly reduce the risk of atherosclerosis and related heart conditions.

Healthcare providers often measure cholesterol levels using a blood test called a lipid panel. This test provides information on total cholesterol, LDL cholesterol, HDL cholesterol, and triglycerides (another type of fat in the blood). Ideally, you want to have low levels of LDL and high levels of HDL to minimize the risk of cardiovascular diseases. Total cholesterol should be kept within a healthy range, generally below 200 mg/dL, with LDL levels below 100 mg/dL and HDL levels above 60 mg/dL. However, individual targets may vary based on personal risk factors and overall health.

Lifestyle and Cholesterol Levels

Lifestyle choices play a significant role in managing LDL and HDL cholesterol levels. A diet rich in fruits, vegetables, whole grains, lean proteins, and healthy fats can help improve cholesterol profiles. Foods high in soluble fiber, such as oats, beans, and fruits, can reduce LDL cholesterol by binding to it in the digestive system and preventing its absorption. Omega-3 fatty acids, found in fatty fish like salmon and mackerel, also contribute to lower LDL levels and higher HDL levels.

Regular physical activity is another critical factor. Exercise helps increase HDL cholesterol and lower LDL cholesterol and triglycerides. Activities such as brisk walking, running, cycling, and swimming are particularly effective. Aim for at least 150 minutes of moderate-intensity exercise or 75 minutes of vigorous-intensity exercise each week to maintain optimal cholesterol levels.

Smoking cessation is crucial for improving HDL cholesterol levels. Smoking lowers HDL and damages the arteries, making them more susceptible to plaque buildup. Quitting smoking can improve HDL levels and overall heart health, reducing the risk of cardiovascular diseases.

Maintaining a healthy weight also contributes to better cholesterol management. Excess weight, particularly around the abdomen, is associated with higher LDL levels and lower HDL levels. Weight loss through a combination of diet and exercise can help improve cholesterol profiles and reduce the risk of heart disease.

Medications and Cholesterol

In some cases, lifestyle changes may not be sufficient to manage cholesterol levels effectively. Healthcare providers may prescribe medications to help lower LDL cholesterol and raise HDL cholesterol. Statins are among the most commonly prescribed medications for lowering LDL levels. They work by inhibiting an enzyme in the liver that is necessary for cholesterol production. Other medications, such as bile acid sequestrants, cholesterol absorption inhibitors, and PCSK9 inhibitors, may also be used depending on individual needs and risk factors.

It's important to work closely with a healthcare provider to determine the most appropriate treatment plan for managing cholesterol levels. Regular monitoring through blood tests and follow-up appointments can help ensure that cholesterol levels remain within a healthy range and reduce the risk of cardiovascular diseases.

Understanding the types of cholesterol and their roles in the body is essential for maintaining heart health. While LDL cholesterol is necessary for transporting cholesterol to cells, excessive levels can lead to plaque buildup and cardiovascular diseases. HDL cholesterol helps counterbalance this effect by removing excess cholesterol from the bloodstream and protecting against heart disease. By adopting a heart-healthy lifestyle, including a balanced diet, regular exercise, smoking cessation, and maintaining a healthy weight, individuals can manage their cholesterol levels effectively and reduce the risk of heart-related conditions. In cases where lifestyle changes are not enough, medications prescribed by healthcare providers can help achieve and maintain healthy cholesterol levels.

Navigating the complexities of cholesterol reveals its vital importance and the delicate balance required for health. Cholesterol, a key component in cellular structures and hormone production, becomes a risk factor when levels of LDL, the so-called "bad" cholesterol, rise excessively. LDL's propensity to deposit cholesterol in the arteries can lead to atherosclerosis and cardiovascular diseases. On the other hand, HDL, or "good" cholesterol, acts as a protective agent by removing excess cholesterol from the bloodstream and facilitating its return to the liver for disposal. This interplay between LDL and HDL underscores the necessity of maintaining an optimal balance. Achieving this balance involves a combination of healthy lifestyle choices, including a nutritious diet, regular exercise, smoking cessation, and weight management. In certain situations, medical interventions may be required to regulate cholesterol levels effectively. Understanding these dynamics empowers individuals to take proactive steps toward safeguarding their heart health and enhancing their quality of life.

Chapter 2: Benefits of a Low Cholesterol Diet

Adopting a low cholesterol diet can be transformative, offering numerous benefits that extend far beyond heart health. By prioritizing nutrient-dense foods and avoiding those high in unhealthy fats, you can experience significant improvements in various aspects of your well-being. From reducing the risk of chronic diseases like diabetes and hypertension to enhancing overall health through better energy levels, improved digestion, and radiant skin, a low cholesterol diet is a holistic approach to achieving a healthier lifestyle. This chapter explores these benefits in detail, demonstrating how such dietary choices can lead to a more vibrant and fulfilling life.

Improvements in heart health

Adopting a low cholesterol diet can profoundly impact heart health, steering the body away from the risks associated with high cholesterol levels. The primary benefit lies in its potential to significantly reduce the likelihood of developing cardiovascular diseases, a leading cause of death worldwide. By understanding the intricate relationship between diet, cholesterol, and heart health, we can appreciate the far-reaching benefits of making conscientious dietary choices.

Cholesterol is a critical factor in the development of heart disease. High levels of low-density lipoprotein (LDL) cholesterol can lead to the buildup of plaque in the arteries, a condition known as atherosclerosis. This buildup narrows the arteries, making it harder for blood to flow through them. When blood flow to the heart is restricted, it can result in angina, a type of chest pain. If an artery becomes completely blocked, it can cause a heart attack. A low cholesterol diet helps prevent these issues by reducing the amount of LDL cholesterol in the bloodstream.

One of the most immediate improvements seen with a low cholesterol diet is a decrease in the levels of LDL cholesterol. This reduction occurs because such a diet limits the intake of foods high in saturated fats and trans fats, which are known to raise LDL levels. Instead, it emphasizes the consumption of healthy fats found in foods like avocados, nuts, and olive oil. These healthy fats can help increase levels of high-density lipoprotein (HDL) cholesterol, which works to remove LDL cholesterol from the bloodstream, further protecting the heart.

A low cholesterol diet also encourages the consumption of foods rich in soluble fiber. Soluble fiber, found in foods such as oats, beans, lentils, and certain fruits, binds to cholesterol in the digestive system and helps remove it from the body. This not only lowers LDL cholesterol but also supports overall digestive health. By integrating these fiber-rich foods into your diet, you can effectively reduce cholesterol levels and enhance heart health.

Moreover, antioxidants play a crucial role in heart health, and a low cholesterol diet typically includes a variety of fruits and vegetables that are rich in these beneficial compounds. Antioxidants help protect the arteries from damage caused by free radicals, unstable molecules that can lead to inflammation and atherosclerosis. By consuming a diet high in antioxidants, you can help maintain the integrity of your arteries and reduce the risk of heart disease.

Beyond reducing cholesterol levels, a low cholesterol diet also helps in managing blood pressure, another critical factor in heart health. High blood pressure can damage the arteries over time, making them more susceptible to plaque buildup. Foods that are part of a low cholesterol diet, such as leafy greens, berries, and whole grains, are often rich in potassium and magnesium, minerals that help regulate blood pressure. By keeping blood pressure within a healthy range, you further decrease the risk of heart-related complications.

Additionally, weight management is a significant benefit of a low cholesterol diet that directly impacts heart health. Being overweight or obese increases the risk of developing high cholesterol and heart disease. A diet that focuses on whole, nutrient-dense foods while avoiding high-calorie, processed foods can help maintain a healthy weight. Losing excess weight has been shown to improve cholesterol levels and reduce the burden on the heart, making it easier for the body to maintain optimal cardiovascular function.

Inflammation is another critical factor in heart health, and a low cholesterol diet can help reduce chronic inflammation in the body. Foods high in saturated and trans fats can promote inflammation, contributing to the development of atherosclerosis. In contrast, a diet rich in anti-inflammatory foods, such as fatty fish, nuts, seeds, and a variety of fruits and vegetables, can help mitigate this risk. By lowering inflammation, you not only protect the heart but also improve overall health and well-being.

Furthermore, adopting a low cholesterol diet often leads to better lifestyle choices overall, creating a positive feedback loop that enhances heart health. For instance, individuals who commit to eating healthier are more likely to engage in regular physical activity, another crucial component of cardiovascular health. Exercise helps improve cholesterol levels, manage weight, and reduce blood pressure, all of which contribute to a healthier heart.

It's also worth noting that a low cholesterol diet can improve endothelial function, which is the ability of the blood vessels to dilate and contract as needed. The endothelium, a thin layer of cells lining the blood vessels, plays a vital role in maintaining vascular health. Diets high in saturated fats can impair endothelial function, leading to reduced blood flow and increased risk of heart disease. Conversely, diets rich in healthy fats, fiber, and antioxidants support endothelial health and ensure proper blood vessel function.

In conclusion, the benefits of a low cholesterol diet for heart health are manifold and substantial. By reducing LDL cholesterol, managing blood pressure, aiding in weight management, reducing inflammation, and improving endothelial function, such a diet provides a comprehensive approach to protecting and enhancing cardiovascular health. Making these dietary changes not only decreases the risk of heart disease but also promotes a healthier, more vibrant life overall. Embracing a low cholesterol diet is a proactive and empowering step towards long-term heart health and well-being.

Reduced risk of chronic diseases

A low cholesterol diet is not only beneficial for heart health but also plays a significant role in reducing the risk of various chronic diseases. By focusing on nutritious, wholesome foods and avoiding those high in unhealthy fats, you can substantially lower your chances of developing conditions such as diabetes, hypertension, and certain types of cancer. The interconnected nature of our body's systems means that what benefits one aspect of health often positively impacts others.

Diabetes, a condition characterized by elevated blood sugar levels, is one chronic disease where a low cholesterol diet can make a profound difference. Diets high in saturated fats and trans fats, often found in processed foods, can lead to insulin resistance, a precursor to type 2 diabetes. Insulin resistance occurs when cells in your muscles, fat, and liver don't respond well to insulin and can't easily take up glucose from your blood. By reducing the intake of these unhealthy fats and focusing on foods rich in fiber, lean proteins, and healthy fats, you can improve your body's insulin sensitivity. Whole grains, legumes, and vegetables, staples of a low cholesterol diet, have low glycemic indices, meaning they cause a slower, more gradual rise in blood sugar levels, thereby reducing the risk of developing diabetes.

Hypertension, or high blood pressure, is another chronic condition that can be mitigated by adhering to a low cholesterol diet. High blood pressure strains the heart and damages arteries, increasing the risk of heart disease and stroke. Foods high in cholesterol and unhealthy fats can exacerbate hypertension by contributing to arterial plaque buildup and increasing blood pressure. Conversely, a diet rich in fruits, vegetables, whole grains, and low-fat dairy products can help lower blood pressure. These foods are naturally low in sodium and high in potassium, a mineral that helps balance the amount of sodium in your cells and reduce blood pressure. Moreover, the emphasis on plant-based foods provides ample antioxidants and anti-inflammatory compounds, which further support vascular health and reduce hypertension risk.

Certain types of cancer are also linked to high cholesterol and diets rich in unhealthy fats. Research has shown that high levels of cholesterol may promote the growth and spread of cancer cells. For example, elevated cholesterol levels have been associated with an increased risk of breast, prostate, and colon cancers. A low cholesterol diet, which includes plenty of fruits, vegetables, and whole grains, provides a variety of antioxidants, vitamins, and minerals that help protect cells from damage and reduce cancer risk. These foods contain phytochemicals, naturally occurring compounds in plants, that have been shown to inhibit the growth of cancer cells and prevent the formation of carcinogens.

In addition to diabetes, hypertension, and cancer, a low cholesterol diet can also help manage and prevent obesity, a significant risk factor for many chronic diseases. Obesity is often a consequence of consuming high-calorie, low-nutrient foods, many of which are high in unhealthy fats and added sugars. By focusing on nutrient-dense foods that are low in unhealthy fats, a low cholesterol diet can help regulate body weight. Foods such as lean proteins, whole grains, fruits, and vegetables are filling and satisfying, reducing the likelihood of overeating and promoting a healthy weight. Maintaining a healthy weight reduces the risk of various obesity-related conditions, including type 2 diabetes, heart disease, and certain cancers.

Moreover, a low cholesterol diet supports better kidney function, which is crucial for managing chronic kidney disease (CKD). High cholesterol can lead to the buildup of plaques in the blood vessels supplying the kidneys, reducing their ability to function properly. Over time, this can lead to CKD, a condition where the kidneys gradually lose their ability to filter waste and excess fluids from the blood. By reducing cholesterol intake and focusing on heart-healthy foods, you can improve blood flow to the kidneys and reduce the risk of CKD. Additionally, such a diet often includes foods low in phosphorus and sodium, which are beneficial for kidney health.

Inflammation is a common underlying factor in many chronic diseases, and a low cholesterol diet can help reduce inflammation throughout the body. Chronic inflammation is linked to a wide range of health problems, including arthritis, cardiovascular disease, and autoimmune disorders. Diets high in processed foods, unhealthy fats, and added sugars can trigger inflammatory responses, exacerbating these conditions. In contrast, a diet rich in anti-inflammatory foods, such as fatty fish, nuts, seeds, fruits, and vegetables, can help reduce inflammation. Omega-3 fatty acids, found in fish like salmon and mackerel, are particularly effective at reducing inflammation and improving overall health.

Additionally, a low cholesterol diet can enhance liver health, reducing the risk of non-alcoholic fatty liver disease (NAFLD). NAFLD occurs when too much fat builds up in liver cells, often due to poor diet and lifestyle choices. This condition can lead to liver inflammation and scarring, increasing the risk of liver damage and cirrhosis. By reducing the intake of unhealthy fats and focusing on nutrient-dense, low-cholesterol foods, you can prevent fat accumulation in the liver and support its function. Foods high in antioxidants, such as berries and leafy greens, also help protect the liver from damage and promote detoxification.

Finally, mental health can also benefit from a low cholesterol diet. Emerging research suggests a link between diet and mental health conditions such as depression and anxiety. Diets high in unhealthy fats and sugars can negatively impact brain function and mood. Conversely, a diet rich in omega-3 fatty acids, antioxidants, and other nutrients supports brain health and cognitive function. Healthy fats, found in foods like fish, nuts, and seeds, are essential for maintaining the structure and function of brain cells. Additionally, fruits and vegetables provide vitamins and minerals that support neurotransmitter function, reducing the risk of depression and anxiety.

In conclusion, the benefits of a low cholesterol diet extend far beyond heart health, offering protection against a variety of chronic diseases. By reducing the intake of unhealthy fats and focusing on nutrient-dense foods, you can significantly lower your risk of diabetes, hypertension, certain cancers, obesity, chronic kidney disease, and more. This holistic approach to eating not only supports physical health but also enhances mental well-being, making it a powerful tool for achieving and maintaining overall health and longevity.

Additional benefits to overall health

Adopting a low cholesterol diet doesn't just protect your heart or reduce your risk of chronic diseases; it extends a wealth of benefits that enhance your overall health and well-being. This holistic approach to eating impacts various aspects of physical and mental health, leading to a higher quality of life. By prioritizing nutritious, whole foods and minimizing harmful fats, you can experience significant improvements in energy levels, digestive health, skin condition, and even cognitive function.

One of the most immediate and noticeable benefits of a low cholesterol diet is the boost in energy levels. Foods that are high in unhealthy fats and sugars often lead to energy spikes followed by crashes, making it difficult to maintain consistent energy throughout the day. In contrast, a diet rich in whole grains, lean proteins, fruits, and vegetables provides a steady source of energy. These foods release glucose gradually into the bloodstream, ensuring a consistent supply of fuel for your body and brain. Complex carbohydrates found in foods like oats, quinoa, and sweet potatoes are particularly effective in maintaining stable energy levels, preventing the sluggishness that comes from consuming processed, high-fat foods.

Digestive health also significantly benefits from a low cholesterol diet. Foods high in fiber, such as fruits, vegetables, whole grains, and legumes, promote healthy digestion by aiding in the regularity of bowel movements and preventing constipation. Fiber acts as a bulking agent, helping to move waste through the digestive system efficiently. Moreover, a fiber-rich diet supports a healthy gut microbiome, the community of bacteria living in your intestines. These beneficial bacteria play a crucial role in digestion, immune function, and even mood regulation. By feeding these microbes with high-fiber foods, you enhance their ability to maintain gut health and overall well-being.

Skin health is another area positively impacted by a low cholesterol diet. The nutrients found in a variety of fruits and vegetables, such as vitamins A, C, and E, are essential for maintaining healthy skin. These vitamins have antioxidant properties that protect the skin from damage caused by free radicals, reducing signs of aging and promoting a youthful appearance. Healthy fats from sources like avocados, nuts, and seeds also support skin health by keeping it hydrated and supple. Omega-3 fatty acids, in particular, have anti-inflammatory properties that can help manage conditions like acne and eczema. By consuming a diet rich in these nutrients, you can achieve clearer, more radiant skin.

Mental health benefits are increasingly recognized as another advantage of a low cholesterol diet. The brain is composed largely of fat, and consuming healthy fats is essential for maintaining its structure and function. Omega-3 fatty acids, found in fatty fish, flaxseeds, and walnuts, are crucial for cognitive function and mental health. These fats help build cell membranes in the brain and reduce inflammation, which has been linked to depression and anxiety. Additionally, a diet rich in antioxidants and vitamins supports neurotransmitter function, improving mood and cognitive performance. Studies have shown that individuals who follow a diet high in fruits, vegetables, and healthy fats are less likely to experience depression and anxiety than those who consume a diet high in processed foods and unhealthy fats.

Weight management is another crucial benefit of a low cholesterol diet that contributes to overall health. By focusing on nutrient-dense foods that are low in unhealthy fats and calories, you can maintain a healthy weight more easily. This not only reduces the risk of developing obesity-related conditions but also improves physical mobility and reduces strain on joints. Achieving and maintaining a healthy weight enhances energy levels, self-esteem, and overall quality of life.

Furthermore, a low cholesterol diet supports a strong immune system. Nutrient-rich foods like fruits, vegetables, whole grains, and lean proteins provide the vitamins and minerals necessary for immune function. Vitamin C, found in citrus fruits, bell peppers, and strawberries, boosts the production of white blood cells, which are vital for fighting infections. Zinc, present in foods like beans, nuts, and whole grains, supports immune cell function and wound healing. By consuming a balanced diet rich in these nutrients, you can enhance your body's ability to fend off illnesses and recover more quickly from infections.

Bone health also benefits from a low cholesterol diet. Foods high in calcium and vitamin D, such as leafy greens, fortified plant-based milks, and fatty fish, support bone density and strength. A diet low in unhealthy fats and high in these bone-building nutrients can help prevent osteoporosis and reduce the risk of fractures. Additionally, magnesium and phosphorus, found in nuts, seeds, and whole grains, are essential for maintaining bone health. By ensuring that your diet includes these vital nutrients, you can support skeletal health and prevent bone-related issues as you age.

Moreover, a low cholesterol diet can improve reproductive health. Healthy fats are crucial for the production of hormones involved in reproduction. Consuming a balanced diet that includes healthy fats from sources like avocados, nuts, and seeds can help regulate hormone levels and improve fertility. Additionally, antioxidants and vitamins found in fruits and vegetables support reproductive health by protecting cells from damage and improving overall function. By maintaining a diet rich in these nutrients, you can support reproductive health and increase the likelihood of a healthy pregnancy.

In conclusion, a low cholesterol diet offers a myriad of benefits that extend beyond heart health and the reduction of chronic disease risk. From boosting energy levels and improving digestive health to enhancing skin condition, mental health, and weight management, the advantages are comprehensive and far-reaching. This approach to eating not only supports physical health but also contributes to mental and emotional well-being, leading to a higher quality of life. By embracing a low cholesterol diet, you invest in a healthier, more vibrant future, enjoying the full spectrum of benefits that come from nourishing your body with wholesome, nutrient-dense foods.

The benefits of a low cholesterol diet are extensive and profound, impacting every aspect of your health. By reducing LDL cholesterol levels, this diet helps prevent heart disease and promotes cardiovascular wellness. Beyond heart health, it lowers the risk of chronic conditions such as diabetes, hypertension, and certain cancers, offering a protective shield against some of the most common health issues. Additionally, a low cholesterol diet supports overall well-being, enhancing energy levels, improving digestive health, and contributing to clearer skin and better mental health. These changes collectively lead to weight management and stronger immune and bone health, showcasing the holistic advantages of this dietary approach. Embracing a low cholesterol diet is a powerful step toward a healthier, more balanced life, providing the foundation for long-term well-being and vitality.

Chapter 3: Principles of a Low Cholesterol Diet

Embracing a low cholesterol diet involves making strategic choices about the foods you include and avoid. Understanding these principles is crucial for effectively managing cholesterol levels and promoting heart health. By focusing on nutrient-rich foods that support cardiovascular wellness and steering clear of those that contribute to high cholesterol and related health issues, you can transform your diet into a powerful tool for maintaining overall well-being. This chapter delves into the specific foods that should be part of your daily regimen and highlights those to limit or avoid to achieve optimal health.

Foods to include

Adopting a low cholesterol diet begins with understanding which foods to incorporate into your daily meals. The focus should be on nutrient-dense, whole foods that promote heart health and overall well-being. By choosing the right foods, you can effectively lower your cholesterol levels and reduce the risk of cardiovascular diseases. Here, we delve into the key food groups and specific items that should be staples in your low cholesterol diet.

Fruits and Vegetables

Fruits and vegetables are foundational to any healthy diet, and they play a crucial role in managing cholesterol levels. Rich in vitamins, minerals, fiber, and antioxidants, these foods help reduce LDL cholesterol and improve overall heart health. Soluble fiber, in particular, is effective at lowering cholesterol. It binds to cholesterol in the digestive system and helps remove it from the body. Apples, oranges, strawberries, and grapes are excellent sources of soluble fiber. Vegetables such as carrots, Brussels sprouts, and okra also provide significant amounts of this beneficial fiber. Moreover, the antioxidants found in fruits and vegetables help protect against the oxidative stress that contributes to heart disease.

Whole Grains

Incorporating whole grains into your diet is another effective strategy for managing cholesterol. Unlike refined grains, whole grains contain all parts of the grain, including the bran, germ, and endosperm, which retain their nutritional value. Whole grains are rich in soluble fiber, which helps lower LDL cholesterol. Oats are particularly renowned for their cholesterol-lowering properties, thanks to a type of soluble fiber called beta-glucan. Other beneficial whole grains include barley, quinoa, brown rice, and whole wheat. These grains not only help reduce cholesterol but also provide sustained energy and improve digestive health.

Nuts and Seeds

Nuts and seeds are packed with healthy fats, fiber, and protein, making them an excellent addition to a low cholesterol diet. They contain monounsaturated and polyunsaturated fats, which are heart-healthy fats that help lower LDL cholesterol and raise HDL cholesterol. Almonds, walnuts, flaxseeds, chia seeds, and sunflower seeds are all great choices. These nuts and seeds also provide omega-3 fatty acids, which have anti-inflammatory properties and support overall cardiovascular health. Including a handful of nuts or a sprinkle of seeds in your meals can make a significant difference in your cholesterol levels.

Legumes

Legumes, such as beans, lentils, and peas, are excellent sources of plant-based protein and fiber. They are low in saturated fat and cholesterol-free, making them ideal for a heart-healthy diet. The soluble fiber in legumes helps lower LDL cholesterol, while their high protein content makes them a satisfying alternative to animal-based proteins, which are often higher in cholesterol and saturated fats. Incorporating legumes into your diet can be as simple as adding lentils to soups, beans to salads, or chickpeas to stews. They are versatile, nutritious, and beneficial for maintaining healthy cholesterol levels.

Fatty Fish

Fatty fish, such as salmon, mackerel, sardines, and trout, are rich in omega-3 fatty acids, which are essential for heart health. Omega-3s help lower triglycerides, reduce inflammation, and raise HDL cholesterol levels. Eating fatty fish at least twice a week is recommended for its cardiovascular benefits. Grilling, baking, or steaming fish are healthy preparation methods that retain its nutritional value without adding unhealthy fats. For those who do not consume fish, omega-3 supplements derived from algae can be a suitable alternative.

Healthy Oils

Replacing saturated fats with healthy oils is a key principle of a low cholesterol diet. Olive oil, in particular, is high in monounsaturated fats, which help lower LDL cholesterol. Extra virgin olive oil, being the least processed, retains more of its beneficial compounds, including antioxidants. Avocado oil and canola oil are also good options, providing healthy fats without contributing to cholesterol levels. These oils can be used in cooking, salad dressings, and as a replacement for butter or margarine.

Soy Products

Soy products, such as tofu, tempeh, and edamame, are excellent plant-based protein sources that can help reduce cholesterol levels. Soy contains compounds called isoflavones, which have been shown to lower LDL cholesterol. Replacing animal-based proteins with soy products can significantly impact cholesterol management. Incorporating soy milk, tofu stir-fries, or edamame snacks into your diet can provide the benefits of soy without adding cholesterol or saturated fat.

Tea

Certain beverages, like tea, can also contribute to a low cholesterol diet. Green tea and black tea contain antioxidants called catechins and theaflavins, respectively, which help lower LDL cholesterol. Regular consumption of these teas can provide a beneficial boost to heart health. Opting for unsweetened tea is best to avoid added sugars that can negate the health benefits.

Dark Chocolate

In moderation, dark chocolate can be part of a heart-healthy diet. Dark chocolate contains flavonoids, antioxidants that help improve heart health by lowering blood pressure, improving blood flow, and reducing LDL cholesterol. Choosing dark chocolate with a high cocoa content (70% or higher) and consuming it in small amounts can provide these benefits without excessive calories or sugar.

In summary, a low cholesterol diet is built on a foundation of nutrient-dense, whole foods that support heart health and overall well-being. By prioritizing fruits, vegetables, whole grains, nuts, seeds, legumes, fatty fish, healthy oils, soy products, tea, and even a bit of dark chocolate, you can effectively manage your cholesterol levels and enjoy a varied, flavorful diet. Embracing these foods not only helps lower LDL cholesterol but also provides a wealth of other health benefits, contributing to a balanced and healthful lifestyle.

Foods to avoid

Navigating a low cholesterol diet involves not only embracing healthy foods but also understanding which foods to avoid. Certain items can significantly raise your cholesterol levels and increase the risk of heart disease. By being mindful of these dietary pitfalls, you can make more informed choices that support your overall health and well-being.

Saturated Fats

Saturated fats are a primary culprit in raising LDL cholesterol levels. These fats are typically solid at room temperature and are found in animal products such as red meat, butter, cheese, and full-fat dairy products. When consumed in excess, saturated fats can cause the liver to produce more LDL cholesterol, which then circulates in the blood and contributes to plaque buildup in the arteries. To maintain healthy cholesterol levels, it is essential to limit the intake of foods high in saturated fats. Opt for leaner cuts of meat, choose low-fat or fat-free dairy options, and use healthier fat alternatives like olive oil instead of butter.

Trans Fats

Trans fats are even more harmful than saturated fats and should be completely avoided whenever possible. These artificial fats are created through a process called hydrogenation, which turns liquid oils into solid fats. Trans fats are commonly found in processed foods, such as baked goods, snack foods, margarine, and fried foods. They not only raise LDL cholesterol but also lower HDL cholesterol, creating a double whammy effect on heart health. Additionally, trans fats can increase inflammation and contribute to insulin resistance. Carefully read food labels and avoid any product that lists partially hydrogenated oils in the ingredients.

Processed Meats

Processed meats, such as bacon, sausage, hot dogs, and deli meats, are typically high in saturated fats and cholesterol. These foods are also often loaded with sodium and preservatives, which can contribute to hypertension and other health issues. Regular consumption of processed meats has been linked to an increased risk of heart disease and certain cancers. Instead of processed meats, opt for fresh, lean protein sources like chicken, turkey, fish, and plant-based proteins such as beans and legumes.

Fried Foods

Fried foods are another major source of unhealthy fats, particularly trans fats, and should be avoided to maintain healthy cholesterol levels. Foods like French fries, fried chicken, and doughnuts are often cooked in oils that contain trans fats. Even when trans fats are not present, the high levels of saturated fats and calories in fried foods can still negatively impact heart health. Baking, grilling, steaming, or roasting are healthier cooking methods that do not add unnecessary fats to your meals.

Baked Goods and Sweets

Many baked goods and sweets, such as cookies, cakes, pastries, and pies, are high in both saturated fats and trans fats. These foods also often contain large amounts of added sugars, which can contribute to weight gain, insulin resistance, and increased triglyceride levels. High triglyceride levels can further exacerbate the risk of heart disease. When you crave something sweet, choose healthier alternatives like fresh fruit or homemade treats made with healthier ingredients like whole grains and natural sweeteners.

Full-Fat Dairy Products

While dairy can be part of a healthy diet, full-fat dairy products are high in saturated fats and should be limited. Foods like whole milk, cream, full-fat yogurt, and cheese can raise LDL cholesterol levels if consumed in large quantities. Opt for low-fat or fat-free versions of these products to enjoy the nutritional benefits of dairy without the negative impact on cholesterol levels. Plant-based dairy alternatives, such as almond milk, soy milk, or oat milk, can also be excellent substitutes.

Fast Food

Fast food is notoriously high in unhealthy fats, sodium, and calories, making it a significant contributor to high cholesterol levels and heart disease. Items like burgers, fries, fried chicken, and pizza often contain high amounts of saturated and trans fats. Additionally, the portion sizes are usually large, leading to excessive calorie consumption. Reducing your intake of fast food and preparing meals at home with fresh, whole ingredients can make a substantial difference in your cholesterol management and overall health.

High-Cholesterol Foods

Certain foods are naturally high in cholesterol and should be consumed in moderation or avoided, especially if you have high cholesterol levels. These include organ meats like liver, shellfish such as shrimp and lobster, and egg yolks. While dietary cholesterol's impact on blood cholesterol levels varies from person to person, it is generally advisable to limit the intake of these foods. Egg whites, lean cuts of meat, and plant-based protein sources are healthier alternatives.

Snack Foods

Many popular snack foods, such as chips, crackers, and microwave popcorn, are high in unhealthy fats and sodium. These snacks often contain trans fats and are calorie-dense but nutrient-poor. Choosing healthier snacks like raw vegetables, fruits, nuts, and seeds can help you avoid the pitfalls of unhealthy snacking while still satisfying your hunger between meals.

Sugary Beverages

Sugary beverages, including soda, sweetened coffee drinks, and fruit juices with added sugars, can contribute to weight gain and increased triglyceride levels, negatively impacting heart health. These drinks often provide empty calories with little to no nutritional value. Opting for water, herbal teas, or beverages with no added sugars can help you maintain a healthier diet and better manage your cholesterol levels.

Adopting the principles of a low cholesterol diet requires a thoughtful approach to food selection, focusing on choices that nourish and protect your heart. Incorporating fruits, vegetables, whole grains, nuts, seeds, legumes, fatty fish, healthy oils, soy products, and even a bit of dark chocolate ensures you receive the nutrients essential for lowering LDL cholesterol and supporting overall health. Simultaneously, avoiding foods high in saturated and trans fats, processed meats, fried foods, sugary beverages, and other unhealthy options is vital for preventing cholesterol buildup and reducing the risk of cardiovascular diseases. By making these informed dietary decisions, you not only manage your cholesterol levels but also embrace a lifestyle that fosters long-term health, vitality, and well-being. This balanced approach to eating empowers you to take control of your health and enjoy the numerous benefits of a heart-healthy diet.

In conclusion, being mindful of the foods you avoid is just as crucial as knowing what to include in a low cholesterol diet. By steering clear of saturated fats, trans fats, processed meats, fried foods, baked goods, full-fat dairy, fast food, high-cholesterol foods, unhealthy snack foods, and sugary beverages, you can significantly improve your cholesterol levels and overall heart health. Making these dietary changes requires conscious effort and commitment, but the benefits to your long-term health and well-being are well worth it. Embracing a diet rich in whole, nutrient-dense foods while avoiding these harmful options sets the foundation for a healthier, more vibrant life.

Chapter 4: Low Cholesterol Breakfasts

Easy recipes to get your day off to a good start

1. Avocado and Tomato Toast

Preparation time: 5 minutes | **Cooking time:** 5 minutes | **Portions:** 2

Difficulty: Easy

Ingredients:

- 2 slices of whole wheat bread
- 1 ripe avocado
- 1 medium tomato, sliced
- 1 tbsp olive oil
- A pinch of sea salt and black pepper

Preparation:

1. Toast the whole wheat bread slices until golden brown.
2. Halve the avocado, remove the pit, and scoop out the flesh into a bowl. Mash the avocado with a fork until smooth.
3. Spread the mashed avocado evenly on each slice of toast.
4. Arrange the tomato slices on top of the avocado spread.
5. Drizzle with olive oil and season with sea salt and black pepper to taste.

Nutritional values (per serving): Calories 250 | Fat 18g | Carbohydrates 20g | Protein 5g

2. Berry Overnight Oats

Preparation time: 10 minutes (plus overnight refrigeration) | **Cooking time:** 0 minutes | **Portions:** 2

Difficulty: Easy

Ingredients:

- 1 cup rolled oats
- 1 cup almond milk
- 1/2 cup mixed berries (blueberries, raspberries, strawberries)
- 2 tbsp chia seeds
- 1 tbsp honey

Preparation:

1. In a medium bowl, combine the rolled oats, almond milk, mixed berries, chia seeds, and honey.
2. Stir well to mix all the ingredients.
3. Divide the mixture into two jars or containers.
4. Refrigerate overnight to allow the oats and chia seeds to absorb the liquid.
5. In the morning, give it a good stir and enjoy straight from the jar.

Nutritional values (per serving): Calories 300 | Fat 10g | Carbohydrates 48g | Protein 7g

3. Spinach and Mushroom Egg White Omelette

Preparation time: 10 minutes | **Cooking time:** 10 minutes | **Portions:** 2

Difficulty: Medium

Ingredients:

- 6 egg whites
- 1 cup fresh spinach, chopped
- 1/2 cup mushrooms, sliced
- 1 tbsp olive oil
- A pinch of salt and pepper

Preparation:

1. Heat olive oil in a non-stick skillet over medium heat.
2. Add the mushrooms and cook until they start to brown, about 3-4 minutes.
3. Add the chopped spinach and cook until wilted, about 2 minutes.
4. Pour in the egg whites and let them set slightly before stirring gently.
5. Cook until the eggs are fully set, then fold the omelette in half.
6. Season with salt and pepper to taste.

Nutritional values (per serving): Calories 120 | Fat 5g | Carbohydrates 4g | Protein 16g

4. Greek Yogurt with Fresh Berries and Honey

Preparation time: 5 minutes | **Cooking time:** 0 minutes | **Portions:** 2

Difficulty: Easy

Ingredients:

- 1 cup Greek yogurt (low-fat)
- 1/2 cup mixed fresh berries (blueberries, raspberries, strawberries)
- 1 tbsp honey
- 1 tbsp chia seeds

Preparation:

1. Divide the Greek yogurt into two bowls.
2. Top each bowl with the mixed fresh berries.
3. Drizzle with honey.
4. Sprinkle with chia seeds.

Nutritional values (per serving): Calories 150 | Fat 3g | Carbohydrates 25g | Protein 10g

5. Quinoa Breakfast Bowl with Almonds and Bananas

Preparation time: 10 minutes | **Cooking time:** 15 minutes | **Portions:** 2

Difficulty: Medium

Ingredients:

- 1/2 cup quinoa
- 1 cup almond milk
- 1 banana, sliced
- 2 tbsp sliced almonds
- 1 tbsp honey

Preparation:

1. Rinse the quinoa under cold water.
2. In a small pot, bring the almond milk to a boil.
3. Add the quinoa and reduce the heat to low. Cover and simmer for 15 minutes or until the quinoa is cooked and the liquid is absorbed.
4. Divide the cooked quinoa into two bowls.
5. Top with sliced banana, almonds, and a drizzle of honey.

Nutritional values (per serving): Calories 280 | Fat 10g | Carbohydrates 45g | Protein 6g

6. Whole Grain Pancakes with Blueberry Compote

Preparation time: 10 minutes | **Cooking time:** 15 minutes | **Portions:** 2

Difficulty: Medium

Ingredients:

- 1 cup whole grain pancake mix
- 1/2 cup water
- 1 cup blueberries
- 1 tbsp maple syrup
- 1 tsp lemon zest

Preparation:

1. Prepare the pancake mix according to the package instructions, using water.
2. Heat a non-stick skillet over medium heat and pour the batter to form pancakes. Cook until bubbles form on the surface, then flip and cook until golden brown.
3. In a small pot, combine blueberries, maple syrup, and lemon zest. Cook over medium heat until the blueberries burst and form a compote.
4. Serve the pancakes topped with blueberry compote.

Nutritional values (per serving): Calories 220 | Fat 2g | Carbohydrates 48g | Protein 6g

7. Chia Seed Pudding with Mango

Preparation time: 5 minutes (plus overnight refrigeration) | **Cooking time:** 0 minutes | **Portions:** 2

Difficulty: Easy

Ingredients:

- 1/4 cup chia seeds
- 1 cup coconut milk
- 1 mango, diced
- 1 tbsp honey

Preparation:

1. In a medium bowl, combine chia seeds and coconut milk. Stir well.
2. Refrigerate overnight to allow the chia seeds to gel.
3. Divide the pudding into two bowls.
4. Top with diced mango and a drizzle of honey.

Nutritional values (per serving): Calories 250 | Fat 15g | Carbohydrates 29g | Protein 5g

8. Apple and Cinnamon Steel-Cut Oats

Preparation time: 5 minutes | **Cooking time:** 20 minutes | **Portions:** 2
Difficulty: Medium
Ingredients:

- 1 cup steel-cut oats
- 2 cups water
- 1 apple, diced
- 1 tsp ground cinnamon
- 1 tbsp maple syrup

Preparation:

1. Bring water to a boil in a medium pot.
2. Add steel-cut oats and reduce the heat to a simmer. Cook for 15-20 minutes, stirring occasionally, until the oats are tender.
3. Stir in diced apple and ground cinnamon.
4. Divide into two bowls and drizzle with maple syrup.

Nutritional values (per serving): Calories 220 | Fat 3g | Carbohydrates 42g | Protein 6g

9. Veggie Scramble with Whole Wheat Toast

Preparation time: 10 minutes | **Cooking time:** 10 minutes | **Portions:** 2
Difficulty: Medium
Ingredients:

- 4 eggs
- 1/2 cup bell peppers, diced
- 1/2 cup spinach, chopped
- 1 tbsp olive oil
- 2 slices whole wheat toast

Preparation:

1. Heat olive oil in a non-stick skillet over medium heat.
2. Add bell peppers and cook until softened, about 3 minutes.
3. Add spinach and cook until wilted, about 2 minutes.
4. Beat the eggs in a bowl, then pour into the skillet. Cook, stirring gently, until the eggs are set.
5. Serve with whole wheat toast.

Nutritional values (per serving): Calories 300 | Fat 18g | Carbohydrates 20g | Protein 18g

10. Smoked Salmon and Avocado Bagel

Preparation time: 5 minutes | **Cooking time:** 5 minutes | **Portions:** 2

Difficulty: Easy

Ingredients:

- 1 whole wheat bagel, halved
- 1/2 avocado, sliced
- 4 slices smoked salmon
- A pinch of dill
- A squeeze of lemon juice

Preparation:

1. Toast the whole wheat bagel halves.
2. Arrange avocado slices on each bagel half.
3. Top with smoked salmon slices.
4. Sprinkle with dill and a squeeze of lemon juice.

Nutritional values (per serving): Calories 350 | Fat 20g | Carbohydrates 30g | Protein 15g

11. Cottage Cheese with Pineapple and Chia Seeds

Preparation time: 5 minutes | **Cooking time:** 0 minutes | **Portions:** 2

Difficulty: Easy

Ingredients:

- 1 cup low-fat cottage cheese
- 1/2 cup pineapple chunks
- 2 tbsp chia seeds
- 1 tbsp honey

Preparation:

1. Divide the cottage cheese into two bowls.
2. Top each bowl with pineapple chunks.
3. Sprinkle chia seeds over the top.
4. Drizzle with honey.

Nutritional values (per serving): Calories 180 | Fat 5g | Carbohydrates 22g | Protein 14g

12. Low-Fat Greek Yogurt Parfait with Granola

Preparation time: 5 minutes | **Cooking time:** 0 minutes | **Portions:** 2
Difficulty: Easy
Ingredients:

- 1 cup low-fat Greek yogurt
- 1/2 cup granola
- 1/2 cup mixed berries (blueberries, raspberries, strawberries)
- 1 tbsp honey

Preparation:

1. In two glasses, layer Greek yogurt, granola, and mixed berries.
2. Drizzle with honey.

Nutritional values (per serving): Calories 250 | Fat 6g | Carbohydrates 38g | Protein 12g

13. Whole Wheat English Muffin with Peanut Butter and Banana

Preparation time: 5 minutes | **Cooking time:** 5 minutes | **Portions:** 2
Difficulty: Easy
Ingredients:

- 1 whole wheat English muffin, split
- 2 tbsp peanut butter
- 1 banana, sliced
- A pinch of cinnamon

Preparation:

1. Toast the English muffin halves.
2. Spread peanut butter on each half.
3. Top with banana slices.
4. Sprinkle with cinnamon.

Nutritional values (per serving): Calories 280 | Fat 12g | Carbohydrates 34g | Protein 8g

14. Tomato and Basil Frittata

Preparation time: 10 minutes | **Cooking time:** 15 minutes | **Portions:** 2
Difficulty: Medium
Ingredients:

- 4 eggs
- 1/2 cup cherry tomatoes, halved
- 1/4 cup fresh basil leaves, chopped
- 1 tbsp olive oil
- A pinch of salt and pepper

Preparation:

1. Preheat the oven to 375°F (190°C).
2. In a bowl, beat the eggs and season with salt and pepper.
3. Heat olive oil in an oven-safe skillet over medium heat.
4. Add cherry tomatoes and cook for 2-3 minutes.
5. Pour the beaten eggs into the skillet and sprinkle with basil.
6. Cook until the edges begin to set, then transfer the skillet to the oven.
7. Bake for 10-12 minutes, or until the frittata is fully set.

Nutritional values (per serving): Calories 200 | Fat 14g | Carbohydrates 4g | Protein 12g

15. Oatmeal with Sliced Almonds and Dried Cranberries

Preparation time: 5 minutes | **Cooking time:** 10 minutes | **Portions:** 2
Difficulty: Easy
Ingredients:

- 1 cup rolled oats
- 2 cups water
- 1/4 cup sliced almonds
- 1/4 cup dried cranberries
- 1 tbsp maple syrup

Preparation:

1. In a medium pot, bring water to a boil.
2. Add rolled oats, reduce heat to low, and simmer for 5-7 minutes, stirring occasionally.
3. Divide the oatmeal into two bowls.
4. Top with sliced almonds, dried cranberries, and a drizzle of maple syrup.

Nutritional values (per serving): Calories 280 | Fat 10g | Carbohydrates 45g | Protein 7g

16. Sweet Potato and Black Bean Breakfast Burrito

Preparation time: 10 minutes | **Cooking time:** 15 minutes | **Portions:** 2

Difficulty: Medium

Ingredients:

- 1 medium sweet potato, peeled and diced
- 1/2 cup black beans, drained and rinsed
- 2 whole wheat tortillas
- 1 tbsp olive oil
- 1/2 tsp cumin
- A pinch of salt and pepper

Preparation:

1. Heat olive oil in a skillet over medium heat.
2. Add sweet potato and cook until tender, about 10 minutes.
3. Add black beans, cumin, salt, and pepper. Cook for another 5 minutes.
4. Warm the tortillas in a dry skillet or microwave.
5. Divide the sweet potato and black bean mixture between the tortillas and wrap to form burritos.

Nutritional values (per serving): Calories 300 | Fat 8g | Carbohydrates 52g | Protein 8g

17. Lemon Ricotta Pancakes

Preparation time: 10 minutes | **Cooking time:** 15 minutes | **Portions:** 2

Difficulty: Medium

Ingredients:

- 1 cup ricotta cheese
- 2 eggs
- 1/2 cup whole wheat flour
- 1 lemon, zested
- 1 tbsp honey

Preparation:

1. In a bowl, mix ricotta cheese, eggs, whole wheat flour, lemon zest, and honey until smooth.
2. Heat a non-stick skillet over medium heat.
3. Pour 1/4 cup of batter for each pancake into the skillet.
4. Cook until bubbles form on the surface, then flip and cook until golden brown.
5. Serve warm.

Nutritional values (per serving): Calories 280 | Fat 12g | Carbohydrates 28g | Protein 14g

18. Zucchini and Carrot Muffins

Preparation time: 10 minutes | **Cooking time:** 20 minutes | **Portions:** 2

Difficulty: Medium

Ingredients:

- 1 cup whole wheat flour
- 1/2 cup grated zucchini
- 1/2 cup grated carrot
- 1 egg
- 1/4 cup olive oil
- 1 tbsp honey

Preparation:

1. Preheat the oven to 350°F (175°C).
2. In a bowl, mix whole wheat flour, grated zucchini, grated carrot, egg, olive oil, and honey until well combined.
3. Divide the batter into a greased muffin tin.
4. Bake for 18-20 minutes or until a toothpick inserted into the center comes out clean.

Nutritional values (per serving): Calories 220 | Fat 10g | Carbohydrates 28g | Protein 5g

19. Tofu Scramble with Spinach and Mushrooms

Preparation time: 10 minutes | **Cooking time:** 10 minutes | **Portions:** 2

Difficulty: Medium

Ingredients:

*   1 block firm tofu, drained and crumbled
*   1 cup spinach, chopped
*   1/2 cup mushrooms, sliced
*   1 tbsp olive oil
*   1/2 tsp turmeric
*   A pinch of salt and pepper

Preparation:

1. Heat olive oil in a skillet over medium heat.
2. Add mushrooms and cook until they begin to soften, about 3-4 minutes.
3. Add crumbled tofu, turmeric, salt, and pepper. Cook for 5 minutes.
4. Add spinach and cook until wilted, about 2 minutes.
5. Serve hot.

Nutritional values (per serving): Calories 200 | Fat 12g | Carbohydrates 8g | Protein 18g

20. Green Tea Infused Oatmeal

Preparation time: 5 minutes | **Cooking time:** 10 minutes | **Portions:** 2

Difficulty: Easy

Ingredients:

- 1 cup rolled oats
- 2 cups brewed green tea
- 1 tbsp honey
- 1/4 cup almonds, chopped

Preparation:

1. In a medium pot, bring brewed green tea to a boil.
2. Add rolled oats, reduce heat to low, and simmer for 5-7 minutes, stirring occasionally.
3. Divide the oatmeal into two bowls.
4. Drizzle with honey and top with chopped almonds.

Nutritional values (per serving): Calories 220 | Fat 8g | Carbohydrates 35g | Protein 6g

Smoothies and Quick Options

21. Green Detox Smoothie

Preparation time: 5 minutes | **Cooking time:** 0 minutes | **Portions:** 2

Difficulty: Easy

Ingredients:

- 2 cups spinach
- 1 green apple, cored and chopped
- 1 banana
- 1 cup coconut water
- 1 tbsp chia seeds

Preparation:

1. Combine spinach, green apple, banana, coconut water, and chia seeds in a blender.
2. Blend until smooth.
3. Pour into glasses and serve immediately.

Nutritional values (per serving): Calories 150 | Fat 3g | Carbohydrates 30g | Protein 3g

22. Berry Blast Smoothie

Preparation time: 5 minutes | **Cooking time:** 0 minutes | **Portions:** 2

Difficulty: Easy

Ingredients:

- 1 cup mixed berries (blueberries, raspberries, strawberries)
- 1 banana
- 1 cup almond milk
- 1 tbsp flaxseeds

Preparation:

1. Combine mixed berries, banana, almond milk, and flaxseeds in a blender.
2. Blend until smooth.
3. Pour into glasses and serve immediately.

Nutritional values (per serving): Calories 180 | Fat 4g | Carbohydrates 35g | Protein 3g

23. Tropical Mango Smoothie

Preparation time: 5 minutes | **Cooking time:** 0 minutes | **Portions:** 2

Difficulty: Easy

Ingredients:

- 1 cup mango chunks
- 1/2 cup pineapple chunks
- 1 banana
- 1 cup coconut milk
- 1 tbsp honey

Preparation:

1. Combine mango, pineapple, banana, coconut milk, and honey in a blender.
2. Blend until smooth.
3. Pour into glasses and serve immediately.

Nutritional values (per serving): Calories 220 | Fat 8g | Carbohydrates 40g | Protein 2g

24. Spinach and Avocado Smoothie

Preparation time: 5 minutes | **Cooking time:** 0 minutes | **Portions:** 2

Difficulty: Easy

Ingredients:

- 2 cups spinach
- 1 avocado, peeled and pitted
- 1 banana
- 1 cup almond milk
- 1 tbsp honey

Preparation:

1. Combine spinach, avocado, banana, almond milk, and honey in a blender.
2. Blend until smooth.
3. Pour into glasses and serve immediately.

Nutritional values (per serving): Calories 250 | Fat 15g | Carbohydrates 30g | Protein 3g

25. Pineapple and Kale Smoothie

Preparation time: 5 minutes | **Cooking time:** 0 minutes | **Portions:** 2

Difficulty: Easy

Ingredients:

- 1 cup pineapple chunks
- 1 cup kale leaves, stems removed
- 1 banana
- 1 cup coconut water
- 1 tbsp chia seeds

Preparation:

1. Combine pineapple, kale, banana, coconut water, and chia seeds in a blender.
2. Blend until smooth.
3. Pour into glasses and serve immediately.

Nutritional values (per serving): Calories 160 | Fat 4g | Carbohydrates 30g | Protein 2g

26. Blueberry and Almond Milk Smoothie

Preparation time: 5 minutes | **Cooking time:** 0 minutes | **Portions:** 2

Difficulty: Easy

Ingredients:

- 1 cup blueberries
- 1 banana
- 1 cup almond milk
- 1 tbsp almond butter

Preparation:

1. Combine blueberries, banana, almond milk, and almond butter in a blender.
2. Blend until smooth.
3. Pour into glasses and serve immediately.

Nutritional values (per serving): Calories 180 | Fat 8g | Carbohydrates 25g | Protein 4g

27. Strawberry Banana Smoothie

Preparation time: 5 minutes | **Cooking time:** 0 minutes | **Portions:** 2

Difficulty: Easy

Ingredients:

- 1 cup strawberries
- 1 banana
- 1 cup Greek yogurt (low-fat)
- 1 tbsp honey

Preparation:

1. Combine strawberries, banana, Greek yogurt, and honey in a blender.
2. Blend until smooth.
3. Pour into glasses and serve immediately.

Nutritional values (per serving): Calories 220 | Fat 3g | Carbohydrates 40g | Protein 10g

28. Apple and Carrot Smoothie

Preparation time: 5 minutes | **Cooking time:** 0 minutes | **Portions:** 2

Difficulty: Easy

Ingredients:

- 1 apple, cored and chopped
- 1 carrot, peeled and chopped
- 1 banana
- 1 cup orange juice
- 1 tbsp honey

Preparation:

1. Combine apple, carrot, banana, orange juice, and honey in a blender.
2. Blend until smooth.
3. Pour into glasses and serve immediately.

Nutritional values (per serving): Calories 180 | Fat 1g | Carbohydrates 45g | Protein 2g

29. Beetroot and Ginger Smoothie

Preparation time: 5 minutes | **Cooking time:** 0 minutes | **Portions:** 2

Difficulty: Easy

Ingredients:

- 1 medium beetroot, peeled and chopped
- 1 banana
- 1/2 inch piece of fresh ginger
- 1 cup coconut water
- 1 tbsp honey

Preparation:

1. Combine beetroot, banana, ginger, coconut water, and honey in a blender.
2. Blend until smooth.
3. Pour into glasses and serve immediately.

Nutritional values (per serving): Calories 150 | Fat 1g | Carbohydrates 35g | Protein 2g

30. Protein-Packed Smoothie with Chia Seeds

Preparation time: 5 minutes | **Cooking time:** 0 minutes | **Portions:** 2

Difficulty: Easy

Ingredients:

- 1 cup almond milk
- 1 banana
- 2 tbsp chia seeds
- 1 tbsp almond butter
- 1 scoop protein powder (optional)

Preparation:

1. Combine almond milk, banana, chia seeds, almond butter, and protein powder in a blender.
2. Blend until smooth.
3. Pour into glasses and serve immediately.

Nutritional values (per serving): Calories 220 | Fat 10g | Carbohydrates 25g | Protein 10g

Chapter 5: Healthy Lunches

Tasty and nutritious recipes for lunch

31. Grilled Chicken and Quinoa Salad

Preparation time: 15 minutes | **Cooking time:** 20 minutes | **Portions:** 2
Difficulty: Medium
Ingredients:

- 1/2 cup quinoa
- 1 cup water
- 1 chicken breast, grilled and sliced
- 1 cup mixed greens
- 1/2 cup cherry tomatoes, halved
- 1 tbsp olive oil
- 1 tbsp lemon juice

Preparation:

1. Rinse quinoa under cold water. In a small pot, bring water to a boil, add quinoa, reduce heat to low, cover, and simmer for 15 minutes or until water is absorbed.
2. In a large bowl, combine cooked quinoa, grilled chicken, mixed greens, and cherry tomatoes.
3. Drizzle with olive oil and lemon juice. Toss to combine and serve.

Nutritional values (per serving): Calories 350 | Fat 15g | Carbohydrates 30g | Protein 25g

32. Lentil and Vegetable Soup

Preparation time: 15 minutes | **Cooking time:** 30 minutes | **Portions:** 2

Difficulty: Medium

Ingredients:

- 1/2 cup lentils
- 4 cups vegetable broth
- 1 carrot, diced
- 1 celery stalk, diced
- 1 onion, chopped
- 1 tbsp olive oil

Preparation:

1. Heat olive oil in a large pot over medium heat. Add carrot, celery, and onion; cook until vegetables are tender, about 5 minutes.
2. Add lentils and vegetable broth. Bring to a boil, then reduce heat and simmer for 25-30 minutes until lentils are tender.
3. Season with salt and pepper to taste. Serve hot.

Nutritional values (per serving): Calories 220 | Fat 5g | Carbohydrates 35g | Protein 12g

33. Chickpea and Spinach Stew

Preparation time: 10 minutes | **Cooking time:** 20 minutes | **Portions:** 2

Difficulty: Medium

Ingredients:

- 1 can chickpeas, drained and rinsed
- 2 cups spinach, chopped
- 1 onion, chopped
- 2 garlic cloves, minced
- 1 tbsp olive oil
- 1 tsp cumin

Preparation:

1. Heat olive oil in a large skillet over medium heat. Add onion and garlic; cook until softened, about 5 minutes.
2. Add chickpeas and cumin; cook for another 5 minutes.
3. Add spinach and cook until wilted, about 5 minutes. Season with salt and pepper to taste. Serve hot.

Nutritional values (per serving): Calories 220 | Fat 8g | Carbohydrates 30g | Protein 10g

34. Grilled Veggie Wrap with Hummus

Preparation time: 10 minutes | **Cooking time:** 15 minutes | **Portions:** 2

Difficulty: Medium

Ingredients:

- 2 whole wheat tortillas
- 1/2 cup hummus
- 1 zucchini, sliced
- 1 red bell pepper, sliced
- 1/2 eggplant, sliced
- 1 tbsp olive oil

Preparation:

1. Heat olive oil in a grill pan over medium heat. Grill zucchini, bell pepper, and eggplant slices until tender, about 5-7 minutes per side.
2. Spread hummus evenly over each tortilla.
3. Arrange grilled vegetables on top and roll up the tortillas tightly. Cut in half and serve.

Nutritional values (per serving): Calories 300 | Fat 12g | Carbohydrates 40g | Protein 8g

35. Turkey and Avocado Sandwich

Preparation time: 10 minutes | **Cooking time:** 0 minutes | **Portions:** 2

Difficulty: Easy

Ingredients:

- 4 slices whole grain bread
- 4 oz sliced turkey breast
- 1 avocado, sliced
- 1 tomato, sliced
- 1 tbsp mustard

Preparation:

1. Spread mustard on each slice of bread.
2. Layer turkey, avocado, and tomato slices on two slices of bread.
3. Top with the remaining bread slices, cut in half, and serve.

Nutritional values (per serving): Calories 350 | Fat 15g | Carbohydrates 35g | Protein 20g

36. Asian-Inspired Tofu Salad

Preparation time: 15 minutes | **Cooking time:** 10 minutes | **Portions:** 2

Difficulty: Medium

Ingredients:

- 1 block firm tofu, cubed
- 1 tbsp soy sauce
- 1 tbsp sesame oil
- 1 cup mixed greens
- 1/2 cup shredded carrots
- 1/4 cup sliced almonds

Preparation:

1. Heat sesame oil in a skillet over medium heat. Add tofu cubes and cook until golden brown, about 5-7 minutes.
2. In a large bowl, combine mixed greens, shredded carrots, and tofu.
3. Drizzle with soy sauce and sprinkle with sliced almonds. Toss to combine and serve.

Nutritional values (per serving): Calories 300 | Fat 18g | Carbohydrates 20g | Protein 15g

37. Greek Salad with Lemon Vinaigrette

Preparation time: 10 minutes | **Cooking time:** 0 minutes | **Portions:** 2

Difficulty: Easy

Ingredients:

- 1 cucumber, chopped
- 1 tomato, chopped
- 1/2 red onion, sliced
- 1/4 cup Kalamata olives
- 1/4 cup feta cheese, crumbled
- 1 tbsp olive oil
- 1 tbsp lemon juice

Preparation:

1. In a large bowl, combine cucumber, tomato, red onion, olives, and feta cheese.
2. Drizzle with olive oil and lemon juice. Toss to combine and serve.

Nutritional values (per serving): Calories 200 | Fat 15g | Carbohydrates 10g | Protein 5g

38. Black Bean and Corn Salad

Preparation time: 10 minutes | **Cooking time:** 0 minutes | **Portions:** 2

Difficulty: Easy

Ingredients:

- 1 can black beans, drained and rinsed
- 1 cup corn kernels (fresh or frozen, thawed)
- 1 red bell pepper, diced
- 1/4 cup cilantro, chopped
- 1 tbsp lime juice

Preparation:

1. In a large bowl, combine black beans, corn, bell pepper, and cilantro.
2. Drizzle with lime juice and toss to combine. Serve chilled.

Nutritional values (per serving): Calories 220 | Fat 3g | Carbohydrates 40g | Protein 10g

39. Zucchini Noodles with Pesto

Preparation time: 10 minutes | **Cooking time:** 5 minutes | **Portions:** 2

Difficulty: Medium

Ingredients:

- 2 zucchinis, spiralized into noodles
- 1/4 cup pesto sauce
- 1 tbsp olive oil
- 1 clove garlic, minced
- 1/4 cup cherry tomatoes, halved

Preparation:

1. Heat olive oil in a skillet over medium heat. Add garlic and cook until fragrant, about 1 minute.
2. Add zucchini noodles and cook for 2-3 minutes until just tender.
3. Remove from heat and toss with pesto sauce.
4. Top with cherry tomatoes and serve.

Nutritional values (per serving): Calories 200 | Fat 15g | Carbohydrates 10g | Protein 3g

40. Tomato and Basil Soup

Preparation time: 10 minutes | **Cooking time:** 30 minutes | **Portions:** 2
Difficulty: Medium
Ingredients:

- 4 cups tomatoes, chopped
- 1 onion, chopped
- 2 cloves garlic, minced
- 2 cups vegetable broth
- 1/4 cup fresh basil leaves, chopped
- 1 tbsp olive oil

Preparation:

1. Heat olive oil in a large pot over medium heat. Add onion and garlic; cook until softened, about 5 minutes.
2. Add tomatoes and vegetable broth. Bring to a boil, then reduce heat and simmer for 20 minutes.
3. Use an immersion blender to blend the soup until smooth.
4. Stir in fresh basil and season with salt and pepper. Serve hot.

Nutritional values (per serving): Calories 150 | Fat 5g | Carbohydrates 25g | Protein 3g

41. Spinach and Strawberry Salad with Poppy Seed Dressing

Preparation time: 10 minutes | **Cooking time:** 0 minutes | **Portions:** 2
Difficulty: Easy
Ingredients:

- 4 cups baby spinach
- 1 cup strawberries, sliced
- 1/4 cup almonds, sliced
- 1/4 cup feta cheese, crumbled
- 2 tbsp poppy seed dressing

Preparation:

1. In a large bowl, combine baby spinach, strawberries, almonds, and feta cheese.
2. Drizzle with poppy seed dressing and toss gently to combine.
3. Serve immediately.

Nutritional values (per serving): Calories 220 | Fat 15g | Carbohydrates 18g | Protein 6g

42. Baked Falafel with Tahini Sauce

Preparation time: 15 minutes | **Cooking time:** 25 minutes | **Portions:** 2

Difficulty: Medium

Ingredients:

- 1 can chickpeas, drained and rinsed
- 1/4 cup fresh parsley, chopped
- 1/2 onion, chopped
- 2 cloves garlic, minced
- 2 tbsp olive oil
- 2 tbsp tahini

Preparation:

1. Preheat oven to 375°F (190°C).
2. In a food processor, combine chickpeas, parsley, onion, garlic, and 1 tbsp olive oil. Pulse until mixture is well combined but still slightly chunky.
3. Form the mixture into small patties and place on a greased baking sheet.
4. Brush the patties with the remaining olive oil and bake for 20-25 minutes, flipping halfway through, until golden brown.
5. Serve with a drizzle of tahini sauce.

Nutritional values (per serving): Calories 250 | Fat 15g | Carbohydrates 25g | Protein 7g

43. Stuffed Bell Peppers with Quinoa

Preparation time: 15 minutes | **Cooking time:** 30 minutes | **Portions:** 2
Difficulty: Medium
Ingredients:

- 2 bell peppers, halved and seeded
- 1/2 cup quinoa
- 1 cup vegetable broth
- 1/2 cup black beans, drained and rinsed
- 1/4 cup corn kernels
- 1 tbsp olive oil

Preparation:

1. Preheat oven to 375°F (190°C).
2. In a small pot, bring vegetable broth to a boil. Add quinoa, reduce heat to low, cover, and simmer for 15 minutes or until liquid is absorbed.
3. In a large bowl, combine cooked quinoa, black beans, corn, and olive oil.
4. Stuff each bell pepper half with the quinoa mixture and place in a baking dish.
5. Cover with foil and bake for 25-30 minutes until peppers are tender.

Nutritional values (per serving): Calories 250 | Fat 8g | Carbohydrates 40g | Protein 8g

44. Cucumber and Dill Yogurt Salad

Preparation time: 10 minutes | **Cooking time:** 0 minutes | **Portions:** 2
Difficulty: Easy
Ingredients:

- 1 cucumber, thinly sliced
- 1 cup Greek yogurt (low-fat)
- 1/4 cup fresh dill, chopped
- 1 tbsp lemon juice
- A pinch of salt and pepper

Preparation:

1. In a large bowl, combine cucumber slices, Greek yogurt, dill, lemon juice, salt, and pepper.
2. Mix well to combine.
3. Serve chilled.

Nutritional values (per serving): Calories 100 | Fat 3g | Carbohydrates 12g | Protein 8g

45. Mixed Greens with Grilled Shrimp

Preparation time: 10 minutes | **Cooking time:** 10 minutes | **Portions:** 2

Difficulty: Medium

Ingredients:

- 1/2 lb shrimp, peeled and deveined
- 4 cups mixed greens
- 1/2 cup cherry tomatoes, halved
- 1/4 cup red onion, sliced
- 1 tbsp olive oil
- 1 tbsp lemon juice

Preparation:

1. Preheat grill to medium-high heat.
2. Toss shrimp with olive oil and season with salt and pepper.
3. Grill shrimp for 2-3 minutes per side until pink and cooked through.
4. In a large bowl, combine mixed greens, cherry tomatoes, and red onion.
5. Top with grilled shrimp and drizzle with lemon juice. Toss to combine and serve.

Nutritional values (per serving): Calories 250 | Fat 10g | Carbohydrates 12g | Protein 28g

46. Roasted Beet and Arugula Salad

Preparation time: 15 minutes | **Cooking time:** 45 minutes | **Portions:** 2

Difficulty: Medium

Ingredients:

- 2 beets, roasted and sliced
- 4 cups arugula
- 1/4 cup goat cheese, crumbled
- 1/4 cup walnuts, toasted

- 2 tbsp balsamic vinegar

Preparation:

1. Preheat oven to 400°F (200°C). Wrap beets in foil and roast for 45 minutes until tender. Let cool, then peel and slice.
2. In a large bowl, combine arugula, roasted beets, goat cheese, and walnuts.
3. Drizzle with balsamic vinegar and toss gently to combine.
4. Serve immediately.

Nutritional values (per serving): Calories 220 | Fat 14g | Carbohydrates 18g | Protein 6g

47. Avocado and Black Bean Tacos

Preparation time: 10 minutes | **Cooking time:** 5 minutes | **Portions:** 2
Difficulty: Easy
Ingredients:

- 4 small corn tortillas
- 1 avocado, sliced
- 1 cup black beans, drained and rinsed
- 1/2 cup corn kernels
- 1 tbsp lime juice

Preparation:

1. Warm tortillas in a dry skillet over medium heat for about 1 minute per side.
2. In a medium bowl, combine black beans, corn, and lime juice.
3. Divide the black bean mixture among the tortillas.
4. Top with avocado slices and serve immediately.

Nutritional values (per serving): Calories 300 | Fat 12g | Carbohydrates 40g | Protein 8g

48. Vegetable Sushi Rolls

Preparation time: 15 minutes | **Cooking time:** 10 minutes | **Portions:** 2
Difficulty: Medium
Ingredients:

- 1 cup sushi rice, cooked
- 4 nori sheets
- 1/2 cucumber, julienned
- 1/2 carrot, julienned

- 1 avocado, sliced

Preparation:

1. Place a nori sheet on a bamboo sushi mat.
2. Spread a thin layer of sushi rice over the nori, leaving a 1-inch border at the top.
3. Arrange cucumber, carrot, and avocado slices in a line across the center of the rice.
4. Roll the sushi tightly using the mat, then slice into pieces.
5. Repeat with remaining ingredients and serve.

Nutritional values (per serving): Calories 250 | Fat 10g | Carbohydrates 35g | Protein 4g

49. Whole Wheat Pasta Salad with Cherry Tomatoes and Feta

Preparation time: 10 minutes | **Cooking time:** 10 minutes | **Portions:** 2

Difficulty: Easy

Ingredients:

- 2 cups whole wheat pasta, cooked
- 1 cup cherry tomatoes, halved
- 1/4 cup feta cheese, crumbled
- 1/4 cup fresh basil, chopped
- 1 tbsp olive oil

Preparation:

1. In a large bowl, combine cooked pasta, cherry tomatoes, feta cheese, and fresh basil.
2. Drizzle with olive oil and toss to combine.
3. Serve chilled or at room temperature.

Nutritional values (per serving): Calories 300 | Fat 12g | Carbohydrates 40g | Protein 10g

50. Kale and Sweet Potato Salad

Preparation time: 15 minutes | **Cooking time:** 20 minutes | **Portions:** 2

Difficulty: Medium

Ingredients:

- 1 large sweet potato, peeled and cubed
- 4 cups kale, chopped
- 1/4 cup dried cranberries
- 1/4 cup pecans, chopped
- 1 tbsp olive oil

Preparation:

1. Preheat oven to 400°F (200°C). Toss sweet potato cubes with 1/2 tbsp olive oil and roast for 20 minutes until tender.

2. In a large bowl, combine kale, roasted sweet potato, dried cranberries, and pecans.

3. Drizzle with remaining olive oil and toss to combine.

4. Serve immediately.

Nutritional values (per serving): Calories 250 | Fat 10g | Carbohydrates 35g | Protein 5g

Chapter 6: Healthy and Flavorful Dinners

Evening meals the whole family will enjoy

51. Baked Lemon Herb Salmon

Preparation time: 10 minutes | **Cooking time:** 20 minutes | **Portions:** 2

Difficulty: Medium

Ingredients:

- 2 salmon fillets
- 1 lemon, sliced
- 1 tbsp olive oil
- 1 tsp dried dill
- 1 tsp garlic powder

Preparation:

1. Preheat oven to 375°F (190°C).
2. Place salmon fillets on a baking sheet lined with parchment paper.
3. Drizzle with olive oil and sprinkle with dill and garlic powder.
4. Arrange lemon slices on top of the salmon.
5. Bake for 20 minutes or until salmon is cooked through and flakes easily with a fork.

Nutritional values (per serving): Calories 300 | Fat 18g | Carbohydrates 3g | Protein 30g

52. Quinoa-Stuffed Bell Peppers

Preparation time: 15 minutes | **Cooking time:** 30 minutes | **Portions:** 2

Difficulty: Medium

Ingredients:

- 2 bell peppers, halved and seeded
- 1/2 cup quinoa
- 1 cup vegetable broth
- 1/4 cup corn kernels
- 1/4 cup black beans, drained and rinsed
- 1 tbsp olive oil

Preparation:

1. Preheat oven to 375°F (190°C).
2. In a small pot, bring vegetable broth to a boil. Add quinoa, reduce heat to low, cover, and simmer for 15 minutes or until liquid is absorbed.
3. In a large bowl, combine cooked quinoa, corn, black beans, and olive oil.
4. Stuff each bell pepper half with the quinoa mixture and place in a baking dish.
5. Cover with foil and bake for 25-30 minutes until peppers are tender.

Nutritional values (per serving): Calories 250 | Fat 8g | Carbohydrates 40g | Protein 8g

53. Grilled Chicken with Mango Salsa

Preparation time: 15 minutes | **Cooking time:** 20 minutes | **Portions:** 2
Difficulty: Medium
Ingredients:

- 2 chicken breasts
- 1 mango, diced
- 1/4 red onion, finely chopped
- 1/4 cup cilantro, chopped
- 1 tbsp lime juice

Preparation:

1. Preheat grill to medium-high heat.
2. Season chicken breasts with salt and pepper.
3. Grill chicken for 6-8 minutes per side or until cooked through.
4. In a bowl, combine mango, red onion, cilantro, and lime juice.
5. Top grilled chicken with mango salsa and serve.

Nutritional values (per serving): Calories 300 | Fat 8g | Carbohydrates 20g | Protein 40g

54. Vegetarian Chili with Black Beans

Preparation time: 15 minutes | **Cooking time:** 30 minutes | **Portions:** 2
Difficulty: Medium
Ingredients:

- 1 can black beans, drained and rinsed
- 1 can diced tomatoes
- 1/2 cup corn kernels
- 1 bell pepper, diced
- 1 onion, chopped
- 1 tbsp chili powder

Preparation:

1. In a large pot, heat a small amount of oil over medium heat. Add onion and bell pepper, cook until softened, about 5 minutes.
2. Add black beans, diced tomatoes, corn, and chili powder. Stir to combine.
3. Bring to a boil, then reduce heat and simmer for 20-25 minutes.
4. Serve hot.

Nutritional values (per serving): Calories 250 | Fat 4g | Carbohydrates 45g | Protein 12g

55. Baked Cod with a Garlic Herb Crust

Preparation time: 10 minutes | **Cooking time:** 20 minutes | **Portions:** 2

Difficulty: Medium

Ingredients:

- 2 cod fillets
- 1/4 cup whole wheat breadcrumbs
- 1 tbsp fresh parsley, chopped
- 2 garlic cloves, minced
- 1 tbsp olive oil

Preparation:

1. Preheat oven to 375°F (190°C).
2. In a bowl, combine breadcrumbs, parsley, garlic, and olive oil.
3. Place cod fillets on a baking sheet lined with parchment paper.
4. Press the breadcrumb mixture onto the top of each fillet.
5. Bake for 20 minutes or until cod is cooked through and flakes easily with a fork.

Nutritional values (per serving): Calories 220 | Fat 8g | Carbohydrates 10g | Protein 30g

56. Tofu Stir-Fry with Broccoli and Peppers

Preparation time: 10 minutes | **Cooking time:** 15 minutes | **Portions:** 2

Difficulty: Medium

Ingredients:

- 1 block firm tofu, cubed
- 1 cup broccoli florets
- 1 red bell pepper, sliced
- 2 tbsp soy sauce
- 1 tbsp sesame oil

Preparation:

1. Heat sesame oil in a large skillet over medium-high heat.
2. Add tofu and cook until golden brown, about 5-7 minutes.
3. Add broccoli and bell pepper, cook for another 5-7 minutes.
4. Stir in soy sauce and cook for an additional 2 minutes.
5. Serve hot.

Nutritional values (per serving): Calories 220 | Fat 12g | Carbohydrates 12g | Protein 16g

57. Spaghetti Squash with Marinara Sauce

Preparation time: 15 minutes | **Cooking time:** 40 minutes | **Portions:** 2

Difficulty: Medium

Ingredients:

- 1 spaghetti squash
- 2 cups marinara sauce
- 1 tbsp olive oil
- 1/4 cup Parmesan cheese, grated

Preparation:

1. Preheat oven to 375°F (190°C).
2. Cut spaghetti squash in half lengthwise and remove seeds. Drizzle with olive oil.
3. Place squash halves cut side down on a baking sheet. Bake for 40 minutes or until tender.
4. Use a fork to scrape out the spaghetti-like strands from the squash.
5. Heat marinara sauce in a small pot. Divide the squash into two bowls and top with marinara sauce.
6. Sprinkle with Parmesan cheese and serve.

Nutritional values (per serving): Calories 250 | Fat 12g | Carbohydrates 30g | Protein 6g

58. Moroccan Chickpea Stew

Preparation time: 15 minutes | **Cooking time:** 30 minutes | **Portions:** 2
Difficulty: Medium
Ingredients:

- 1 can chickpeas, drained and rinsed
- 1 can diced tomatoes
- 1 carrot, diced
- 1 onion, chopped
- 1 tbsp olive oil
- 1 tsp ground cumin
- 1 tsp ground coriander

Preparation:

1. Heat olive oil in a large pot over medium heat. Add onion and carrot; cook until softened, about 5 minutes.
2. Add chickpeas, diced tomatoes, cumin, and coriander. Stir to combine.
3. Bring to a boil, then reduce heat and simmer for 20-25 minutes.
4. Serve hot.

Nutritional values (per serving): Calories 220 | Fat 8g | Carbohydrates 30g | Protein 10g

59. Roasted Turkey Breast with Sweet Potatoes

Preparation time: 15 minutes | **Cooking time:** 45 minutes | **Portions:** 2

Difficulty: Medium

Ingredients:

- 1 turkey breast
- 2 sweet potatoes, peeled and cubed
- 1 tbsp olive oil
- 1 tsp dried rosemary
- A pinch of salt and pepper

Preparation:

1. Preheat oven to 375°F (190°C).
2. Rub turkey breast with olive oil, rosemary, salt, and pepper.
3. Place turkey breast on a baking sheet. Arrange sweet potato cubes around the turkey.
4. Roast for 45 minutes or until turkey is cooked through and sweet potatoes are tender.
5. Let turkey rest for 10 minutes before slicing. Serve with roasted sweet potatoes.

Nutritional values (per serving): Calories 300 | Fat 8g | Carbohydrates 35g | Protein 28g

60. Vegetable Paella

Preparation time: 15 minutes | **Cooking time:** 30 minutes | **Portions:** 2

Difficulty: Medium

Ingredients:

- 1/2 cup Arborio rice
- 1 cup vegetable broth
- 1/2 cup green peas
- 1 red bell pepper, diced
- 1 tomato, diced
- 1 tbsp olive oil
- 1/2 tsp smoked paprika

Preparation:

1. Heat olive oil in a large skillet over medium heat. Add bell pepper and tomato; cook until softened, about 5 minutes.
2. Add Arborio rice and cook for 2 minutes, stirring constantly.
3. Add vegetable broth and smoked paprika. Bring to a boil, then reduce heat and simmer for 15 minutes.
4. Stir in green peas and cook for an additional 5 minutes until rice is tender and liquid is absorbed.
5. Serve hot.

Nutritional values (per serving): Calories 250 | Fat 8g | Carbohydrates 40g | Protein 5g

61. Grilled Portobello Mushrooms

Preparation time: 10 minutes | **Cooking time:** 15 minutes | **Portions:** 2

Difficulty: Easy

Ingredients:

- 2 large Portobello mushrooms
- 1 tbsp olive oil
- 2 garlic cloves, minced
- 1 tbsp balsamic vinegar
- A pinch of salt and pepper

Preparation:

1. Preheat grill to medium-high heat.
2. In a small bowl, mix olive oil, garlic, balsamic vinegar, salt, and pepper.
3. Brush the mushrooms with the olive oil mixture.
4. Grill mushrooms for 5-7 minutes per side until tender and juicy.
5. Serve hot.

Nutritional values (per serving): Calories 100 | Fat 7g | Carbohydrates 6g | Protein 3g

62. Herb-Crusted Tilapia

Preparation time: 10 minutes | **Cooking time:** 20 minutes | **Portions:** 2

Difficulty: Medium

Ingredients:

- 2 tilapia fillets
- 1/4 cup whole wheat breadcrumbs
- 1 tbsp fresh parsley, chopped
- 2 garlic cloves, minced
- 1 tbsp olive oil

Preparation:

1. Preheat oven to 375°F (190°C).
2. In a small bowl, combine breadcrumbs, parsley, garlic, and olive oil.
3. Place tilapia fillets on a baking sheet lined with parchment paper.
4. Press the breadcrumb mixture onto the top of each fillet.
5. Bake for 20 minutes or until tilapia is cooked through and flakes easily with a fork.

Nutritional values (per serving): Calories 220 | Fat 8g | Carbohydrates 10g | Protein 30g

63. Baked Eggplant Parmesan

Preparation time: 15 minutes | **Cooking time:** 30 minutes | **Portions:** 2

Difficulty: Medium

Ingredients:

- 1 eggplant, sliced into rounds
- 1 cup marinara sauce
- 1/2 cup whole wheat breadcrumbs
- 1/4 cup Parmesan cheese, grated
- 1 tbsp olive oil

Preparation:

1. Preheat oven to 375°F (190°C).
2. Brush eggplant slices with olive oil and dredge in breadcrumbs.
3. Place eggplant slices on a baking sheet and bake for 20 minutes, flipping halfway through.
4. Remove from oven, top with marinara sauce and Parmesan cheese.
5. Return to oven and bake for another 10 minutes until cheese is melted and bubbly.
6. Serve hot.

Nutritional values (per serving): Calories 250 | Fat 10g | Carbohydrates 35g | Protein 10g

64. Chicken and Vegetable Kebabs

Preparation time: 15 minutes | **Cooking time:** 15 minutes | **Portions:** 2

Difficulty: Medium

Ingredients:

- 1 chicken breast, cut into cubes
- 1 red bell pepper, cut into chunks
- 1 zucchini, sliced
- 1 red onion, cut into chunks
- 1 tbsp olive oil

Preparation:

1. Preheat grill to medium-high heat.
2. Thread chicken, bell pepper, zucchini, and onion onto skewers.
3. Brush with olive oil and season with salt and pepper.
4. Grill kebabs for 10-15 minutes, turning occasionally, until chicken is cooked through and vegetables are tender.
5. Serve hot.

Nutritional values (per serving): Calories 250 | Fat 10g | Carbohydrates 12g | Protein 30g

65. Stuffed Acorn Squash

Preparation time: 15 minutes | **Cooking time:** 40 minutes | **Portions:** 2

Difficulty: Medium

Ingredients:

- 1 acorn squash, halved and seeded
- 1/2 cup quinoa
- 1 cup vegetable broth
- 1/4 cup dried cranberries
- 1/4 cup chopped pecans
- 1 tbsp olive oil

Preparation:

1. Preheat oven to 375°F (190°C).
2. Place squash halves cut side down on a baking sheet. Bake for 40 minutes or until tender.
3. In a small pot, bring vegetable broth to a boil. Add quinoa, reduce heat to low, cover, and simmer for 15 minutes or until liquid is absorbed.
4. In a large bowl, combine cooked quinoa, cranberries, pecans, and olive oil.
5. Stuff each squash half with the quinoa mixture and serve.

Nutritional values (per serving): Calories 300 | Fat 12g | Carbohydrates 45g | Protein 6g

66. Slow-Cooked Beef and Vegetable Stew

Preparation time: 20 minutes | **Cooking time:** 6-8 hours (slow cooker) | **Portions:** 2
Difficulty: Medium

Ingredients:

- 1/2 lb beef stew meat
- 2 cups beef broth
- 1 carrot, sliced
- 1 potato, diced
- 1 onion, chopped
- 1 tbsp olive oil

Preparation:

1. Heat olive oil in a skillet over medium heat. Brown the beef stew meat on all sides.
2. Transfer beef to a slow cooker. Add beef broth, carrot, potato, and onion.
3. Cook on low for 6-8 hours until beef is tender and vegetables are cooked.
4. Serve hot.

Nutritional values (per serving): Calories 350 | Fat 18g | Carbohydrates 25g | Protein 25g

67. Shrimp and Avocado Salad

Preparation time: 15 minutes | **Cooking time:** 5 minutes | **Portions:** 2
Difficulty: Easy

Ingredients:

- 1/2 lb shrimp, peeled and deveined
- 1 avocado, sliced
- 4 cups mixed greens
- 1/2 cup cherry tomatoes, halved
- 1 tbsp olive oil
- 1 tbsp lemon juice

Preparation:

1. Heat olive oil in a skillet over medium heat. Cook shrimp until pink and opaque, about 2-3 minutes per side.

2. In a large bowl, combine mixed greens, cherry tomatoes, avocado slices, and cooked shrimp.

3. Drizzle with lemon juice and toss gently to combine.

4. Serve immediately.

Nutritional values (per serving): Calories 300 | Fat 20g | Carbohydrates 12g | Protein 22g

68. Cauliflower Rice Stir-Fry

Preparation time: 10 minutes | **Cooking time:** 10 minutes | **Portions:** 2

Difficulty: Medium

Ingredients:

- 2 cups cauliflower rice
- 1 cup mixed vegetables (carrots, peas, bell pepper)
- 2 tbsp soy sauce
- 1 tbsp sesame oil
- 2 garlic cloves, minced

Preparation:

1. Heat sesame oil in a large skillet over medium-high heat. Add garlic and cook until fragrant, about 1 minute.

2. Add mixed vegetables and cook for 5 minutes until tender.

3. Stir in cauliflower rice and soy sauce. Cook for another 5 minutes until heated through.

4. Serve hot.

Nutritional values (per serving): Calories 150 | Fat 10g | Carbohydrates 12g | Protein 4g

69. Spicy Lentil Curry

Preparation time: 10 minutes | **Cooking time:** 25 minutes | **Portions:** 2
Difficulty: Medium
Ingredients:

- 1 cup red lentils
- 2 cups vegetable broth
- 1 onion, chopped
- 2 garlic cloves, minced
- 1 tbsp curry powder
- 1 tbsp olive oil

Preparation:

1. Heat olive oil in a large pot over medium heat. Add onion and garlic; cook until softened, about 5 minutes.
2. Add curry powder and stir to combine.
3. Add red lentils and vegetable broth. Bring to a boil, then reduce heat and simmer for 20 minutes until lentils are tender.
4. Serve hot.

Nutritional values (per serving): Calories 250 | Fat 8g | Carbohydrates 35g | Protein 12g

70. Balsamic Glazed Chicken

Preparation time: 10 minutes | **Cooking time:** 20 minutes | **Portions:** 2
Difficulty: Medium
Ingredients:

- 2 chicken breasts
- 1/4 cup balsamic vinegar
- 2 tbsp honey
- 1 tbsp olive oil
- 1 garlic clove, minced

Preparation:

1. Preheat oven to 375°F (190°C).
2. In a small bowl, mix balsamic vinegar, honey, olive oil, and garlic.
3. Place chicken breasts in a baking dish and pour the balsamic mixture over them.
4. Bake for 20 minutes or until chicken is cooked through and the glaze is sticky.
5. Serve hot.

Nutritional values (per serving): Calories 300 | Fat 10g | Carbohydrates 20g | Protein 35g

71. Miso-Glazed Salmon

Preparation time: 10 minutes | **Cooking time:** 20 minutes | **Portions:** 2

Difficulty: Medium

Ingredients:

- 2 salmon fillets
- 2 tbsp miso paste
- 1 tbsp soy sauce
- 1 tbsp honey
- 1 tbsp rice vinegar

Preparation:

1. Preheat oven to 375°F (190°C).
2. In a small bowl, mix miso paste, soy sauce, honey, and rice vinegar.
3. Place salmon fillets on a baking sheet lined with parchment paper.
4. Brush the miso mixture over the salmon.
5. Bake for 20 minutes or until salmon is cooked through and flakes easily with a fork.
6. Serve hot.

Nutritional values (per serving): Calories 300 | Fat 18g | Carbohydrates 10g | Protein 30g

72. Zucchini Lasagna

Preparation time: 20 minutes | **Cooking time:** 40 minutes | **Portions:** 2

Difficulty: Medium

Ingredients:

- 2 large zucchinis, sliced lengthwise into thin strips
- 1 cup ricotta cheese
- 1 cup marinara sauce
- 1/2 cup mozzarella cheese, shredded
- 1/4 cup Parmesan cheese, grated

Preparation:

1. Preheat oven to 375°F (190°C).
2. In a baking dish, spread a thin layer of marinara sauce.
3. Layer zucchini strips, ricotta cheese, marinara sauce, and mozzarella cheese.
4. Repeat layers until all ingredients are used, finishing with a layer of mozzarella and Parmesan cheese.
5. Bake for 40 minutes or until bubbly and golden brown.
6. Let cool for 10 minutes before serving.

Nutritional values (per serving): Calories 350 | Fat 20g | Carbohydrates 15g | Protein 25g

73. Turkey Meatballs with Marinara Sauce

Preparation time: 15 minutes | **Cooking time:** 25 minutes | **Portions:** 2

Difficulty: Medium

Ingredients:

- 1/2 lb ground turkey
- 1/4 cup whole wheat breadcrumbs
- 1 egg
- 1/2 cup marinara sauce
- 1 tbsp olive oil

Preparation:

1. Preheat oven to 375°F (190°C).
2. In a bowl, mix ground turkey, breadcrumbs, and egg until well combined.
3. Form mixture into small meatballs and place on a baking sheet.
4. Bake for 20 minutes or until meatballs are cooked through.
5. Heat marinara sauce in a small pot. Add cooked meatballs and simmer for 5 minutes.
6. Serve hot.

Nutritional values (per serving): Calories 300 | Fat 18g | Carbohydrates 15g | Protein 25g

74. Vegan Shepherd's Pie

Preparation time: 20 minutes | **Cooking time:** 40 minutes | **Portions:** 2

Difficulty: Medium

Ingredients:

- 2 potatoes, peeled and diced
- 1 cup lentils, cooked
- 1 cup vegetable broth
- 1 carrot, diced
- 1 onion, chopped
- 1 tbsp olive oil

Preparation:

1. Preheat oven to 375°F (190°C).
2. Boil potatoes in a pot of water until tender. Drain and mash with a little olive oil, salt, and pepper.
3. Heat olive oil in a skillet over medium heat. Add onion and carrot, cook until softened, about 5 minutes.
4. Add cooked lentils and vegetable broth, simmer for 10 minutes.
5. Transfer lentil mixture to a baking dish. Spread mashed potatoes on top.
6. Bake for 20 minutes until golden brown.
7. Serve hot.

Nutritional values (per serving): Calories 300 | Fat 8g | Carbohydrates 50g | Protein 10g

75. Grilled Vegetable Platter with Hummus

Preparation time: 15 minutes | **Cooking time:** 15 minutes | **Portions:** 2

Difficulty: Easy

Ingredients:

- 1 zucchini, sliced
- 1 red bell pepper, sliced
- 1 eggplant, sliced
- 1/2 cup hummus
- 1 tbsp olive oil

Preparation:

1. Preheat grill to medium-high heat.
2. Brush vegetables with olive oil and season with salt and pepper.
3. Grill vegetables for 5-7 minutes per side until tender and grill marks appear.
4. Arrange grilled vegetables on a platter and serve with hummus.

Nutritional values (per serving): Calories 220 | Fat 12g | Carbohydrates 25g | Protein 6g

Chapter 7: Snacks and Snacking

Quick and Easy Recipes

76. Hummus and Veggie Sticks

Preparation time: 10 minutes | **Cooking time:** 0 minutes | **Portions:** 2

Difficulty: Easy

Ingredients:

- 1 cup hummus
- 1 carrot, cut into sticks
- 1 cucumber, cut into sticks
- 1 bell pepper, cut into sticks
- 1 celery stalk, cut into sticks

Preparation:

1. Arrange carrot, cucumber, bell pepper, and celery sticks on a platter.
2. Serve with hummus for dipping.

Nutritional values (per serving): Calories 150 | Fat 8g | Carbohydrates 18g | Protein 4g

77. Baked Sweet Potato Fries

Preparation time: 10 minutes | **Cooking time:** 25 minutes | **Portions:** 2

Difficulty: Easy

Ingredients:

- 2 medium sweet potatoes, peeled and cut into fries
- 1 tbsp olive oil
- 1/2 tsp paprika
- A pinch of salt and pepper

Preparation:

1. Preheat oven to 425°F (220°C).
2. In a large bowl, toss sweet potato fries with olive oil, paprika, salt, and pepper.
3. Arrange fries on a baking sheet in a single layer.
4. Bake for 25 minutes, turning halfway through, until golden and crispy.
5. Serve hot.

Nutritional values (per serving): Calories 200 | Fat 7g | Carbohydrates 32g | Protein 2g

78. Apple Slices with Almond Butter

Preparation time: 5 minutes | **Cooking time:** 0 minutes | **Portions:** 2

Difficulty: Easy

Ingredients:

- 2 apples, sliced
- 4 tbsp almond butter

Preparation:

1. Arrange apple slices on a plate.
2. Serve with almond butter for dipping.

Nutritional values (per serving): Calories 250 | Fat 14g | Carbohydrates 30g | Protein 4g

79. Edamame with Sea Salt

Preparation time: 5 minutes | **Cooking time:** 5 minutes | **Portions:** 2

Difficulty: Easy

Ingredients:

- 2 cups edamame (fresh or frozen)
- 1 tsp sea salt

Preparation:

1. Boil edamame in a pot of water for 5 minutes until tender.
2. Drain and sprinkle with sea salt.
3. Serve warm.

Nutritional values (per serving): Calories 120 | Fat 5g | Carbohydrates 10g | Protein 11g

80. Greek Yogurt Dip with Cucumber Slices

Preparation time: 10 minutes | **Cooking time:** 0 minutes | **Portions:** 2

Difficulty: Easy

Ingredients:

- 1 cup Greek yogurt (low-fat)
- 1 cucumber, sliced
- 1 garlic clove, minced
- 1 tbsp fresh dill, chopped
- A pinch of salt

Preparation:

1. In a bowl, mix Greek yogurt, garlic, dill, and salt.
2. Serve with cucumber slices for dipping.

Nutritional values (per serving): Calories 100 | Fat 3g | Carbohydrates 12g | Protein 8g

81. Roasted Chickpeas

Preparation time: 5 minutes | **Cooking time:** 30 minutes | **Portions:** 2

Difficulty: Easy

Ingredients:

- 1 can chickpeas, drained and rinsed
- 1 tbsp olive oil
- 1/2 tsp smoked paprika
- A pinch of salt and pepper

Preparation:

1. Preheat oven to 400°F (200°C).
2. Pat chickpeas dry with a paper towel.
3. Toss chickpeas with olive oil, smoked paprika, salt, and pepper.
4. Spread chickpeas on a baking sheet in a single layer.
5. Roast for 30 minutes, shaking the pan halfway through, until crispy.
6. Serve hot or at room temperature.

Nutritional values (per serving): Calories 150 | Fat 7g | Carbohydrates 18g | Protein 5g

82. Fresh Fruit Salad

Preparation time: 10 minutes | **Cooking time:** 0 minutes | **Portions:** 2

Difficulty: Easy

Ingredients:

- 1 cup strawberries, sliced
- 1 cup blueberries
- 1 kiwi, peeled and sliced
- 1 banana, sliced
- 1 tbsp honey

Preparation:

1. In a large bowl, combine strawberries, blueberries, kiwi, and banana.
2. Drizzle with honey and toss gently to combine.
3. Serve immediately.

Nutritional values (per serving): Calories 120 | Fat 1g | Carbohydrates 30g | Protein 2g

83. Cottage Cheese with Pineapple

Preparation time: 5 minutes | **Cooking time:** 0 minutes | **Portions:** 2

Difficulty: Easy

Ingredients:

- 1 cup low-fat cottage cheese
- 1/2 cup pineapple chunks

Preparation:

1. Divide cottage cheese into two bowls.
2. Top with pineapple chunks.
3. Serve immediately.

Nutritional values (per serving): Calories 120 | Fat 2g | Carbohydrates 16g | Protein 10g

84. Celery Sticks with Low-Fat Cream Cheese

Preparation time: 5 minutes | **Cooking time:** 0 minutes | **Portions:** 2

Difficulty: Easy

Ingredients:

- 4 celery stalks, cut into sticks
- 4 tbsp low-fat cream cheese

Preparation:

1. Fill each celery stick with low-fat cream cheese.
2. Arrange on a plate and serve.

Nutritional values (per serving): Calories 80 | Fat 4g | Carbohydrates 6g | Protein 4g

85. Air-Popped Popcorn with Nutritional Yeast

Preparation time: 5 minutes | **Cooking time:** 5 minutes | **Portions:** 2

Difficulty: Easy

Ingredients:

- 1/2 cup popcorn kernels
- 1 tbsp nutritional yeast
- 1 tbsp olive oil
- A pinch of salt

Preparation:

1. Air-pop the popcorn kernels according to the manufacturer's instructions.
2. In a large bowl, toss the popcorn with olive oil, nutritional yeast, and salt.
3. Serve immediately.

Nutritional values (per serving): Calories 150 | Fat 7g | Carbohydrates 18g | Protein 3g

86. Avocado Toast Bites

Preparation time: 10 minutes | **Cooking time:** 0 minutes | **Portions:** 2

Difficulty: Easy

Ingredients:

- 1 avocado, mashed
- 4 slices whole grain bread, cut into quarters
- 1 tsp lemon juice
- A pinch of salt and pepper

Preparation:

1. Spread mashed avocado on each bread quarter.
2. Drizzle with lemon juice and season with salt and pepper.
3. Serve immediately.

Nutritional values (per serving): Calories 200 | Fat 12g | Carbohydrates 20g | Protein 4g

87. Mixed Nuts and Dried Fruit Mix

Preparation time: 5 minutes | **Cooking time:** 0 minutes | **Portions:** 2

Difficulty: Easy

Ingredients:

- 1/2 cup mixed nuts (almonds, walnuts, cashews)
- 1/4 cup dried fruit (raisins, cranberries, apricots)

Preparation:

1. Combine mixed nuts and dried fruit in a bowl.
2. Serve immediately or store in an airtight container.

Nutritional values (per serving): Calories 200 | Fat 14g | Carbohydrates 18g | Protein 5g

88. Rice Cakes with Hummus and Cherry Tomatoes

Preparation time: 5 minutes | **Cooking time:** 0 minutes | **Portions:** 2

Difficulty: Easy

Ingredients:

- 4 rice cakes
- 1/2 cup hummus
- 1/2 cup cherry tomatoes, halved

Preparation:

1. Spread hummus on each rice cake.
2. Top with cherry tomato halves.
3. Serve immediately.

Nutritional values (per serving): Calories 150 | Fat 6g | Carbohydrates 20g | Protein 4g

89. Berry and Spinach Smoothie

Preparation time: 5 minutes | **Cooking time:** 0 minutes | **Portions:** 2

Difficulty: Easy

Ingredients:

- 1 cup spinach
- 1 cup mixed berries (blueberries, strawberries, raspberries)
- 1 banana
- 1 cup almond milk

Preparation:

1. Combine spinach, mixed berries, banana, and almond milk in a blender.
2. Blend until smooth.
3. Pour into glasses and serve immediately.

Nutritional values (per serving): Calories 150 | Fat 3g | Carbohydrates 30g | Protein 3g

90. Dark Chocolate and Almonds

Preparation time: 5 minutes | **Cooking time:** 0 minutes | **Portions:** 2

Difficulty: Easy

Ingredients:

- 1/4 cup dark chocolate chips
- 1/4 cup almonds

Preparation:

1. Combine dark chocolate chips and almonds in a bowl.
2. Serve immediately or store in an airtight container.

Nutritional values (per serving): Calories 200 | Fat 14g | Carbohydrates 18g | Protein 4g

Chapter 8: Delicious and Healthy Desserts.

Desserts that satisfy without compromising health

91. Chocolate Avocado Mousse

Preparation time: 10 minutes | **Cooking time:** 0 minutes | **Portions:** 2

Difficulty: Easy

Ingredients:

- 2 ripe avocados
- 1/4 cup unsweetened cocoa powder
- 1/4 cup honey
- 1 tsp vanilla extract

Preparation:

1. Scoop the flesh from the avocados into a blender.
2. Add cocoa powder, honey, and vanilla extract.
3. Blend until smooth and creamy.
4. Divide into serving bowls and chill for 30 minutes before serving.

Nutritional values (per serving): Calories 250 | Fat 18g | Carbohydrates 30g | Protein 3g

92. Berry Chia Seed Pudding

Preparation time: 10 minutes (plus overnight refrigeration) | **Cooking time:** 0 minutes | **Portions:** 2

Difficulty: Easy

Ingredients:

- 1/4 cup chia seeds
- 1 cup almond milk
- 1/2 cup mixed berries
- 1 tbsp honey

Preparation:

1. In a bowl, mix chia seeds, almond milk, and honey.
2. Stir well and let sit for 5 minutes, then stir again.
3. Cover and refrigerate overnight.
4. Serve topped with mixed berries.

Nutritional values (per serving): Calories 200 | Fat 10g | Carbohydrates 25g | Protein 4g

93. Baked Apples with Cinnamon

Preparation time: 10 minutes | **Cooking time:** 30 minutes | **Portions:** 2

Difficulty: Easy

Ingredients:

- 2 apples, cored
- 1 tsp cinnamon
- 1 tbsp honey
- 1/4 cup chopped walnuts

Preparation:

1. Preheat oven to 350°F (175°C).
2. Place apples in a baking dish.
3. Sprinkle with cinnamon, drizzle with honey, and top with walnuts.
4. Bake for 30 minutes or until apples are tender.
5. Serve warm.

Nutritional values (per serving): Calories 180 | Fat 8g | Carbohydrates 28g | Protein 2g

94. Greek Yogurt with Honey and Walnuts

Preparation time: 5 minutes | **Cooking time:** 0 minutes | **Portions:** 2

Difficulty: Easy

Ingredients:

- 1 cup Greek yogurt (low-fat)
- 2 tbsp honey
- 1/4 cup walnuts, chopped

Preparation:

1. Divide Greek yogurt into two bowls.
2. Drizzle each with honey.
3. Top with chopped walnuts and serve.

Nutritional values (per serving): Calories 200 | Fat 10g | Carbohydrates 20g | Protein 10g

95. Banana and Oat Cookies

Preparation time: 10 minutes | **Cooking time:** 15 minutes | **Portions:** 2

Difficulty: Easy

Ingredients:

- 2 ripe bananas, mashed
- 1 cup rolled oats
- 1/4 cup dark chocolate chips

Preparation:

1. Preheat oven to 350°F (175°C).
2. In a bowl, mix mashed bananas and rolled oats.
3. Stir in dark chocolate chips.
4. Drop spoonfuls of dough onto a baking sheet.
5. Bake for 15 minutes until golden brown.
6. Let cool before serving.

Nutritional values (per serving): Calories 200 | Fat 6g | Carbohydrates 36g | Protein 4g

96. Mango Sorbet

Preparation time: 10 minutes (plus freezing time) | **Cooking time:** 0 minutes | **Portions:** 2

Difficulty: Easy

Ingredients:

- 2 ripe mangoes, peeled and diced
- 1 tbsp honey
- 1 tbsp lime juice

Preparation:

1. In a blender, combine mangoes, honey, and lime juice.
2. Blend until smooth.
3. Pour mixture into a freezer-safe container and freeze for at least 2 hours.
4. Scoop into bowls and serve.

Nutritional values (per serving): Calories 120 | Fat 0g | Carbohydrates 30g | Protein 1g

97. Almond Flour Brownies

Preparation time: 15 minutes | **Cooking time:** 25 minutes | **Portions:** 2

Difficulty: Medium

Ingredients:

- 1/2 cup almond flour
- 1/4 cup unsweetened cocoa powder
- 1/4 cup honey
- 1/4 cup coconut oil, melted
- 1 egg

Preparation:

1. Preheat oven to 350°F (175°C).
2. In a bowl, mix almond flour, cocoa powder, honey, coconut oil, and egg until smooth.
3. Pour batter into a greased baking dish.
4. Bake for 25 minutes or until a toothpick inserted into the center comes out clean.
5. Let cool before cutting into squares.

Nutritional values (per serving): Calories 250 | Fat 18g | Carbohydrates 20g | Protein 6g

98. Coconut and Lime Energy Balls

Preparation time: 10 minutes | **Cooking time:** 0 minutes | **Portions:** 2

Difficulty: Easy

Ingredients:

- 1 cup shredded coconut
- 2 tbsp lime juice
- 1 tbsp honey
- 1/4 cup almond flour

Preparation:

1. In a bowl, mix shredded coconut, lime juice, honey, and almond flour until well combined.
2. Roll mixture into small balls.
3. Refrigerate for 30 minutes before serving.

Nutritional values (per serving): Calories 180 | Fat 14g | Carbohydrates 12g | Protein 3g

99. Frozen Yogurt Bark with Berries

Preparation time: 10 minutes (plus freezing time) | **Cooking time:** 0 minutes | **Portions:** 2
Difficulty: Easy
Ingredients:

- 1 cup Greek yogurt (low-fat)
- 1/2 cup mixed berries
- 1 tbsp honey

Preparation:

1. Line a baking sheet with parchment paper.
2. Spread Greek yogurt evenly on the parchment paper.
3. Sprinkle with mixed berries and drizzle with honey.
4. Freeze for at least 2 hours.
5. Break into pieces and serve.

Nutritional values (per serving): Calories 120 | Fat 3g | Carbohydrates 18g | Protein 8g

100. Apple and Blueberry Crisp

Preparation time: 15 minutes | **Cooking time:** 30 minutes | **Portions:** 2
Difficulty: Medium
Ingredients:

- 2 apples, peeled and sliced
- 1/2 cup blueberries
- 1/4 cup rolled oats
- 1/4 cup almond flour
- 1 tbsp honey
- 1 tbsp coconut oil, melted

Preparation:

1. Preheat oven to 350°F (175°C).
2. In a baking dish, combine apples and blueberries.
3. In a bowl, mix rolled oats, almond flour, honey, and coconut oil.
4. Sprinkle oat mixture over the fruit.
5. Bake for 30 minutes until fruit is tender and topping is golden brown.
6. Serve warm.

Nutritional values (per serving): Calories 200 | Fat 8g | Carbohydrates 34g | Protein 3g

101. Dark Chocolate Covered Strawberries

Preparation time: 10 minutes | **Cooking time:** 0 minutes | **Portions:** 2

Difficulty: Easy

Ingredients:

- 1/2 cup dark chocolate chips
- 10 strawberries

Preparation:

1. Melt dark chocolate chips in a microwave-safe bowl, stirring every 30 seconds until smooth.
2. Dip each strawberry into the melted chocolate, coating evenly.
3. Place on a parchment-lined baking sheet and refrigerate until chocolate is set.
4. Serve chilled.

Nutritional values (per serving): Calories 150 | Fat 9g | Carbohydrates 18g | Protein 2g

102. Pineapple and Mint Sorbet

Preparation time: 10 minutes (plus freezing time) | **Cooking time:** 0 minutes | **Portions:** 2
Difficulty: Easy

Ingredients:

- 2 cups pineapple chunks
- 1 tbsp honey
- 1 tbsp fresh mint leaves

Preparation:

1. In a blender, combine pineapple, honey, and mint leaves.
2. Blend until smooth.
3. Pour mixture into a freezer-safe container and freeze for at least 2 hours.
4. Scoop into bowls and serve.

Nutritional values (per serving): Calories 100 | Fat 0g | Carbohydrates 25g | Protein 1g

103. Lemon and Poppy Seed Muffins

Preparation time: 15 minutes | **Cooking time:** 20 minutes | **Portions:** 2
Difficulty: Medium

Ingredients:

- 1/2 cup almond flour
- 1/4 cup Greek yogurt (low-fat)
- 1 egg
- 1/4 cup honey
- 1 tbsp lemon zest
- 1 tbsp poppy seeds

Preparation:

1. Preheat oven to 350°F (175°C).
2. In a bowl, mix almond flour, Greek yogurt, egg, honey, lemon zest, and poppy seeds until smooth.
3. Divide batter into a greased muffin tin.
4. Bake for 20 minutes or until a toothpick inserted into the center comes out clean.
5. Let cool before serving.

Nutritional values (per serving): Calories 180 | Fat 9g | Carbohydrates 18g | Protein 5g

104. Baked Pears with Walnuts

Preparation time: 10 minutes | **Cooking time:** 30 minutes | **Portions:** 2

Difficulty: Easy

Ingredients:

- 2 pears, halved and cored
- 1/4 cup walnuts, chopped
- 1 tbsp honey
- 1/2 tsp cinnamon

Preparation:

1. Preheat oven to 350°F (175°C).
2. Place pear halves in a baking dish.
3. Sprinkle with walnuts, drizzle with honey, and sprinkle with cinnamon.
4. Bake for 30 minutes or until pears are tender.
5. Serve warm.

Nutritional values (per serving): Calories 150 | Fat 8g | Carbohydrates 20g | Protein 2g

105. Raspberry and Almond Parfait

Preparation time: 10 minutes | **Cooking time:** 0 minutes | **Portions:** 2

Difficulty: Easy

Ingredients:

- 1 cup Greek yogurt (low-fat)
- 1/2 cup raspberries
- 1/4 cup almonds, chopped
- 1 tbsp honey

Preparation:

1. In two glasses, layer Greek yogurt, raspberries, and chopped almonds.
2. Drizzle with honey.
3. Serve immediately.

Nutritional values (per serving): Calories 180 | Fat 8g | Carbohydrates 20g | Protein 8g

Chapter 9: Practical Tips for Maintaining the Diet

21-Day Meal Plan

Day	Breakfast	Lunch	Dinner	Snacks	Dessert
1	Avocado and Tomato Toast	Grilled Chicken and Quinoa Salad	Baked Lemon Herb Salmon	Hummus and Veggie Sticks	Chocolate Avocado Mousse
2	Berry Overnight Oats	Lentil and Vegetable Soup	Quinoa-Stuffed Bell Peppers	Baked Sweet Potato Fries	Berry Chia Seed Pudding
3	Spinach and Mushroom Egg White Omelette	Chickpea and Spinach Stew	Grilled Chicken with Mango Salsa	Apple Slices with Almond Butter	Baked Apples with Cinnamon
4	Greek Yogurt with Fresh Berries and Honey	Grilled Veggie Wrap with Hummus	Vegetarian Chili with Black Beans	Edamame with Sea Salt	Greek Yogurt with Honey and Walnuts
5	Quinoa Breakfast Bowl with Almonds and Bananas	Turkey and Avocado Sandwich	Baked Cod with a Garlic Herb Crust	Greek Yogurt Dip with Cucumber Slices	Banana and Oat Cookies
6	Whole Grain Pancakes with Blueberry Compote	Asian-Inspired Tofu Salad	Tofu Stir-Fry with Broccoli and Peppers	Roasted Chickpeas	Mango Sorbet
7	Chia Seed Pudding with Mango	Greek Salad with Lemon Vinaigrette	Spaghetti Squash with Marinara Sauce	Fresh Fruit Salad	Almond Flour Brownies
8	Apple and Cinnamon Steel-Cut Oats	Black Bean and Corn Salad	Moroccan Chickpea Stew	Cottage Cheese with Pineapple	Coconut and Lime Energy Balls
9	Veggie Scramble	Zucchini	Roasted Turkey	Celery Sticks	Frozen Yogurt

	with Whole Wheat Toast	Noodles with Pesto	Breast with Sweet Potatoes	with Low-Fat Cream Cheese	Bark with Berries
10	Smoked Salmon and Avocado Bagel	Tomato and Basil Soup	Vegetable Paella	Air-Popped Popcorn with Nutritional Yeast	Apple and Blueberry Crisp
11	Cottage Cheese with Pineapple and Chia Seeds	Spinach and Strawberry Salad with Poppy Seed Dressing	Grilled Portobello Mushrooms	Avocado Toast Bites	Dark Chocolate Covered Strawberries
12	Low-Fat Greek Yogurt Parfait with Granola	Baked Falafel with Tahini Sauce	Herb-Crusted Tilapia	Mixed Nuts and Dried Fruit Mix	Pineapple and Mint Sorbet
13	Whole Wheat English Muffin with Peanut Butter and Banana	Stuffed Bell Peppers with Quinoa	Eggplant Parmesan (Baked)	Rice Cakes with Hummus and Cherry Tomatoes	Lemon and Poppy Seed Muffins
14	Tomato and Basil Frittata	Cucumber and Dill Yogurt Salad	Chicken and Vegetable Kebabs	Berry and Spinach Smoothie	Baked Pears with Walnuts
15	Oatmeal with Sliced Almonds and Dried Cranberries	Mixed Greens with Grilled Shrimp	Stuffed Acorn Squash	Dark Chocolate and Almonds	Raspberry and Almond Parfait
16	Sweet Potato and Black Bean Breakfast Burrito	Roasted Beet and Arugula Salad	Slow-Cooked Beef and Vegetable Stew	Hummus and Veggie Sticks	Chocolate Avocado Mousse
17	Lemon Ricotta Pancakes	Avocado and Black Bean Tacos	Shrimp and Avocado Salad	Baked Sweet Potato Fries	Berry Chia Seed Pudding

18	Zucchini and Carrot Muffins	Vegetable Sushi Rolls	Cauliflower Rice Stir-Fry	Apple Slices with Almond Butter	Baked Apples with Cinnamon
19	Tofu Scramble with Spinach and Mushrooms	Whole Wheat Pasta Salad with Cherry Tomatoes and Feta	Spicy Lentil Curry	Edamame with Sea Salt	Greek Yogurt with Honey and Walnuts
20	Green Tea Infused Oatmeal	Kale and Sweet Potato Salad	Balsamic Glazed Chicken	Greek Yogurt Dip with Cucumber Slices	Banana and Oat Cookies
21	Green Detox Smoothie	Grilled Chicken and Quinoa Salad	Miso-Glazed Salmon	Roasted Chickpeas	Mango Sorbet

Shopping List

1. Fresh and Vibrant Vegetables:

Ensure your cart is full of colorful, nutrient-rich vegetables. Include leafy greens like spinach, kale, and arugula; vibrant bell peppers; broccoli; carrots; zucchini; cucumbers; tomatoes; sweet potatoes; and eggplant. These vegetables are essential for their vitamins, minerals, and antioxidants, supporting heart health and overall well-being.

2. Whole Grains:

Swap out refined grains for wholesome alternatives. Stock up on quinoa, brown rice, whole wheat pasta, rolled oats, and steel-cut oats. These grains are high in fiber, promoting good digestion and aiding cholesterol management.

3. Lean Proteins:

Choose lean proteins to keep your heart healthy. Opt for skinless poultry (like chicken and turkey), fatty fish (such as salmon and mackerel), tofu, beans, lentils, chickpeas, and eggs. These sources provide essential nutrients without the saturated fats found in other protein options.

4. Heart-Friendly Fats:

Incorporate unsaturated fats into your diet. Add avocados, a variety of nuts (such as almonds, walnuts, and cashews), seeds (chia, flaxseeds, and sunflower seeds), and extra virgin olive oil to your shopping list. These fats can help improve cholesterol levels and support overall heart health.

5. Fruits Bursting with Flavor:

Stock up on an array of fresh fruits. Include berries (blueberries, strawberries, raspberries), citrus fruits (oranges, lemons), apples, pears, bananas, mangoes, and pineapples. These fruits are high in vitamins and antioxidants, making for tasty and nutritious additions to your heart-healthy meals and snacks.

6. Dairy or Dairy Alternatives:

Choose low-fat or fat-free dairy items, and consider plant-based alternatives. Include Greek yogurt, almond milk, coconut milk, and low-fat cottage cheese. These products deliver calcium and vitamin D without the added saturated fats found in full-fat dairy products.

7. Flavorful Herbs and Spices:

Enhance the taste of your dishes with herbs and spices instead of relying on excess salt. Add garlic, ginger, turmeric, cumin, paprika, cinnamon, and herbs like rosemary, thyme, basil, and dill to your shopping list. These not only add flavor but also contribute to heart health.

8. Omega-3 Rich Foods:

Prioritize fatty fish such as salmon, mackerel, and trout for their omega-3 fatty acids. These healthy fats are known to support cardiovascular health. If you prefer a plant-based source, include chia seeds and flaxseeds.

9. Snack Options:

For those mid-day cravings, choose heart-healthy snacks like raw nuts, seeds, fresh fruit, and hummus with veggie sticks. Avoid processed snacks high in salt, sugar, and unhealthy fats. Include air-popped popcorn, rice cakes, and low-fat yogurt for variety.

SCAN THE QR CODE TO DOWNLOAD YOUR BONUS!

Printed in Great Britain
by Amazon

50411067R00057